Tucker-

Thanks for speaking
in my classes this past
year. You're a fun & dynamic
teacher & I'm glad we've
had this chance to work
together!

Happy New Year -
May 2008 be a fantastic
year!

Kryn

ALSO BY KAREN BLUMENTHAL

Six Days in October: The Stock Market Crash of 1929

LETMEPLAY

The Story of Title IX | the law that changed the future of girls in America

Karen Blumenthal

Atheneum Books for Young Readers
New York London Toronto Sydney

ATHENEUM BOOKS FOR YOUNG READERS
An imprint of Simon & Schuster Children's Publishing Division
1230 Avenue of the Americas
New York, New York 10020

Book design by Rita Jules
The text for this book is set in Gotham.

Manufactured in the United States of America
First Edition
10 9 8 7 6 5 4 3 2 1

LIBRARY OF CONGRESS CATALOGING-IN-PUBLICATION DATA
Blumenthal, Karen.
Let me play: the story of Title IX, the law that changed the
future of girls in America / Karen Blumenthal.—1st ed.
p.   cm.
ISBN 0-689-85957-0
[1. Sex discrimination in sports—Law and legislation—United
States—Juvenile literature. 2. Women athletes—Legal status,
laws, etc.—United States—Juvenile literature.] I. Title.
KF166.B58   2005
796' .082—dc22   2004001450

To Abby and Jenny, with love

contents

introduction:
a view from the sidelines

Imagine a time when there were no soccer superstars like Mia Hamm or basketball heroes like Lisa Leslie. Imagine a time when people believed girls shouldn't play team sports at all, but instead should wear only dresses and act like "ladies." Imagine a time when girls were warned that hard math classes were too difficult for them and were told that a college or graduate degree was a waste of time.

Just a generation ago that was the popular thinking. Up until the 1970s there were few school teams or recreation leagues for girls outside of tennis, swimming, and track. At school, boys were encouraged to study math and science to ready them for careers. Girls were supposed to be good in English and prepare to become wives and mothers. The girls who enjoyed math, who might have become engineers or mathematicians, were urged to become teachers. Those who loved science, who dreamed of being veterinarians or doctors, were told that girls should be nurses instead.

Many of the nation's best universities didn't even accept women. Law schools and medical schools had quotas, or limits, on how many women they would take.

Then in the 1960s the civil rights movement inspired a new women's movement, and women began to speak out for fair treatment at school and in the workplace.

For me, one year stood out. As a kid in the 1960s, I had desperately wanted to play basketball. Hour after hour, I shot baskets alone in our driveway—because there was nowhere else to play. In 1972, when I was in seventh grade, a new male teacher arrived who thought girls should have a basketball team. Since hardly any of us had ever played, only seven or eight players signed up. We were short on skills but full of enthusiasm. He had to teach us everything— dribbling, defense, basic rules. In our few games we got stomped. But I loved every minute of it.

1

Above: A Mike Thompson cartoon from the *Detroit Free Press*, 1999.

The year 1972 turned out to be pivotal for many other girls and women. The United States Congress passed several important laws to give girls and women more opportunities. The broadest was the Equal Rights Amendment (ERA), a change to the United States Constitution that would guarantee women the same rights as men. Like my basketball team, the ERA seemed full of promise. But it would face an extremely tough and ultimately unsuccessful fight to win the needed approval of three-fourths of state legislatures.

That same year Congress passed a narrow and modest little law with a bureaucratic name, Title IX. Hardly anyone knew about it, and there wasn't much to it. In a thirty-seven-word introduction, Title IX said that any school receiving money from the government couldn't treat boys and girls differently because of their sex.

Congress wanted girls to be able to take the same math classes as boys, to have a chance to become lawyers and doctors and Ph.D.'s. Before long, Title IX also came to mean that if schools sponsored sports for boys, they should sponsor them for girls, too. For the first time, girls across the United States got a real chance to play on the athletic field—and that little law took on a role far greater than anyone ever imagined it could.

No shots were fired, but a revolution followed, fought by an invisible army of committed activists, parents, coaches, and kids. Within a few short years, tens of thousands of girls were suiting up for basketball, volleyball, and soccer and pouring into colleges and graduate schools. Today, female lawyers, doctors, and Ph.D.s are common. Today, nearly 3 million girls play high school sports, up from only 294,000 in 1971–72. Today, we don't think twice about women playing softball in the Olympics, discovering cancer-causing genes, or serving as federal judges. In three decades Title IX truly changed the lives of girls in America.

Still, the transformation has been painful and difficult. Like most social change, the upheaval wrought by Title IX was complex and messy. Giving something to girls for the first time sometimes meant taking something from boys. To see progress, women and men had to stand up to enormous opposition and endure crushing setbacks. Year after year, the concept that girls should have the same shot as boys has been challenged, in schools, in Congress, and in the U.S. courts.

Even today, Title IX remains one of the nation's most controversial—and important—civil rights laws. And like any law, it can be abolished or changed. Just months before she died in 2002, longtime Title IX advocate Patsy Mink, a U.S. representative from Hawaii, urged Congress to diligently protect the law, warning that those opportunities could be taken away just as quickly as they were created.

How Title IX changed America is, in part, the story of a previous generation. But the final chapter is still being written. Those of you growing up today are still challenging old beliefs about what boys and girls can do and still tearing down barriers. In the years to come the story of Title IX will be your story too.

This is how it started.

This is how it started.

Sports
Illustrated

APRIL 16, 1962   25 CENTS

Donna de Varona
BRILLIANT
GIRL SWIMMER

chapter 1

THE champion

"I feel confident that in the years ahead many of the remaining outmoded barriers to women's aspirations will disappear."
—Eleanor Roosevelt, chairwoman of President John F. Kennedy's Commission on the Status of Women, 1962

Opposite: At just fourteen years old, Donna de Varona graced the cover of *Sports Illustrated* as a world-record holder.

Perched at the starting blocks, about to compete for the United States at the 1964 Olympic Games in Tokyo, Japan, champion swimmer Donna de Varona gathered her thoughts.

Four years earlier, as a tiny thirteen-year-old, she had been the youngest member of the 1960 U.S. Olympic team. At fourteen she was featured on the cover of *Sports Illustrated*. The magazine called her "without question, the best all-around woman swimmer in the world."

Across America many cities were in turmoil as African Americans rallied and demonstrated for basic civil rights. A few women were beginning to speak out for more opportunities.

But Donna's life was a blur of school and sport, including at least four hours of swimming a day, six days a week. Her dad, an insurance salesman, and her mom, who worked at a library, had sacrificed so their second child could shine. The family of six moved to Santa Clara, California,

from Lafayette so Donna could train at a world-class swim club. They scrimped to pay for coaching and trips to swim meets in Japan, Europe, and South America.

Donna's progress was remarkable. By her midteens she had broken numerous U.S. and world records. Most notably, she was the world record holder in the most challenging of swimming events, the 400-meter medley, a grueling combination of butterfly, backstroke, breaststroke, and freestyle laps. Now, at seventeen, she was competing for the ultimate prize: Olympic gold.

Night after night, she had rehearsed this moment just before she went to sleep. "I've got my head on the pillow and I'm in that Tokyo pool. I say to myself, 'What have those seven years of work been for? You know you're in shape. There is no reason anyone should beat you.'"

Donna's first love had not been swimming, but baseball. In elementary school she hurried out after school to join the boys in pickup games. But when the boys moved up to Little League, girls weren't allowed on their teams. All she could do was collect the bats. She quit after one

Above: Intensely focused, Donna de Varona swims the butterfly on the way to a gold medal at the National AAU swimming-and-diving championships in 1964.

That's what I'm here for—
to get that gold medal, boy.
It's free-style. Gung ho. Guts out.

season because "being that close and not being able to play hurt too much."

After her older brother hurt his knee and began swimming as part of his rehabilitation, she followed him to the pool and found her sport. She swam in her first meet at the age of ten.

In the pool she grew into a focused athlete, determined, intense, and competitive. But on dry land she took great pains to look pretty and well dressed like the other girls. After practice in the morning, she would rush to the locker room and sit on the concrete floor, styling her hair under a hooded hair dryer while she ate scrambled eggs from a Thermos.

In the 1960s girls were known as the "weaker" or "fairer" sex, and they were supposed to be dainty, not strong. Very self-conscious about her muscular, sculptured arms, Donna hid them under long sleeves at school. "I really wanted to look feminine," she said.

In the pool, however, she was all strength. When the starter's gun popped in October 1964, she whipped through her two best strokes, the butterfly and the backstroke, and then endured the breaststroke. As she

made the turn for the last leg, she let loose. "I just want to go," she said in *Life* magazine. "That's what I'm here for—to get that gold medal, boy. It's free-style. Gung ho. Guts out."

She won, setting an Olympic record.

Donna returned home as a national hero with two gold medals, one in the medley and another in a 400-meter relay. The Associated Press and United Press International both named her "Most Outstanding Female Athlete of the Year." She was an athlete on top of the world.

Then, suddenly, her swimming career was over.

The best boy swimmers were offered scholarships to continue swimming in college. But there were no such scholarships for the best girls in the world. Few colleges even had any kind of women's sports program. Though she was just a high school senior, "there was no future—no scholarships, no programs, no way I could continue to swim," she said.

Donna knew that if she wanted to be as successful in the world as she had been in the pool, she needed a college education just like the men did—but she would have to pay for it

Above: Donna de Varona holds one of the two gold medals she won at the Tokyo Olympic Games.

herself. Society assumed that educating men was more important than educating women. That realization made her feel like her hard work had been discounted, "that what I'd won seemed somehow cheaper," she said. "It was a devastating feeling."

The experience made her determined to make a difference, to ensure that other girls wouldn't face the same discounted future. Many other women and men were beginning to share a similar determination. Across America too many women were being denied a chance to reach their true potential. Too much precious American talent was being wasted in too many areas. From California to Washington, D.C., they were beginning to call for change.

THE chapter 2 playing field

"I have been far oftener discriminated against because
I am a woman than because I am black."
—Shirley Chisholm, U.S. representative, 1969

The foundation of the United States government, the U.S. Constitution, starts with the simple words "We, the people." But for much of the nation's history, those people were all male. For many years after America was founded, females were considered the property of their fathers or their husbands, not individuals with individual rights.

Left: A 1909 cartoon warns of the troubles that will follow if women won the right to vote.

The first significant step toward changing that view came in 1848, when three hundred women and men gathered in Seneca Falls, New York, to talk about women's rights—or rather, the lack of them. Women couldn't attend college in most states. The wages they earned working outside the home went to their husbands or fathers, not to them. And they were helpless to change the laws because they weren't allowed a vote.

The women at the Seneca Falls Convention drew up a list of demands, and the most controversial was calling for the right to vote. Some Seneca Falls leaders believed the notion was just too outrageous and would overshadow their other demands. But others argued that winning the right to vote for elected officials was crucial. How else could women ever influence laws and the people who made them?

The issue lost its punch during the Civil War, when many supporters turned their attention to ending slavery. After the war ended, black men, including former slaves, were given the right to vote—but *not* black or white women. Many women were outraged, and began to join the women's

Below: Women march for suffrage in 1916.

Failure is impossible!

suffrage movement to fight for the right to vote. But they were up against many more men and women who didn't believe women knew enough to make educated choices and who worried that voting might encourage them to rebel against their husbands and ultimately destroy their families.

Still, the suffragettes would not be stopped. In 1906 Susan B. Anthony gave her last speech to the suffrage group she founded. At a feisty eighty-six years old she rallied the crowd with a determined "Failure is impossible!" She would die soon after, but her words eventually proved prophetic: Fourteen years later, in 1920, the Tennessee legislature became the thirty-sixth to ratify the Nineteenth Amendment to the Constitution. Finally all American women had the opportunity to have a say in their government.

The 1920s and 1930s turned out to be something of a golden time for women. With their power to vote in hand, they became active in a wide variety of social issues, from concerns about child labor to the plight of the poor, splintering their focus into many

directions. They began to enter colleges and graduate schools in record numbers and soon made up nearly half of the students at many universities.

But once again, progress would be derailed by bigger battles. The Great Depression of the 1930s and World War II shifted attention to the pressing issues of poverty at home and tyranny abroad. As men were sent overseas to fight in the 1940s, women began to fill nontraditional jobs. They joined the armed forces as secretaries and nurses and went to work in mills and factories, helping to make munitions and candles and build airplanes. Working side by side with men doing the same jobs, they were paid far less just because they were female.

When the men returned from the war, many women were forced out of their positions and encouraged to return to homemaking. Women who had to keep working, or who simply wanted to work, saw men come in at higher pay. Many women were pushed into lesser positions. The story was always the same: Married women didn't need the same paychecks as

Myra Bradwell: America's First Female Lawyer

As a young woman married to an ambitious lawyer in the 1860s, Myra Bradwell wanted to help out her husband in his law practice. Lawyers in those days didn't go to special law schools. Instead, they studied legal cases and laws and then took a rigorous exam. If they passed, they applied for admission to the state bar.

In 1869, Mrs. Bradwell passed the Illinois bar exam with high honors and turned in her application to practice law. Though she easily qualified, she was turned down because she was a married woman. She filed a lawsuit, but the Illinois Supreme Court turned her down too, saying that her sex was "a sufficient reason for not granting this license."

In one of the nation's early sex discrimination cases she appealed to the U.S. Supreme Court. But America's top court had a different view than she did. "Man is, or should be, woman's protector and defender," the Court wrote in 1873. "The natural and proper timidity and delicacy which belongs to the female sex evidently unfits it for many of the occupations of civil life." It concluded: "The paramount destiny and mission of woman is to fulfill the noble and benign offices of wife and mother. This is the law of the Creator."

Mrs. Bradwell was disappointed by the decision, but her efforts had already made a difference. The Illinois legislature in 1872 opened up professions to both sexes. By then, however, Mrs. Bradwell was too busy to practice law. She had founded and was running the Chicago Legal News, the nation's most popular and influential legal newspaper.

Late in her life, when she was ill with terminal cancer, her husband quietly made a request to the Illinois Supreme Court. In 1890, Myra Bradwell was officially granted a license to practice law, retroactive to 1869, making her America's first female lawyer.

Right: Myra Bradwell, the first female lawyer.

"I've found the job where I fit best!"

FIND YOUR WAR JOB
In Industry – Agriculture – Business

OWI Poster No. 55. Additional copies may be obtained upon request from the Division of Public Inquiries, Office of War Information, Washington, D.C.

Above: A 1943 government poster from World War II encourages women to work to help the war effort.

men because they had husbands to support them. Single women didn't need the same wages because they didn't have families to feed. Over and over, women were told that men were the breadwinners; women were working for just a little extra spending money—even though that was rarely true.

Two dramatic events in the 1950s set off a chain of events that would raise questions about how women were treated. Halfway across the world, the much-feared Soviet Union launched the first man-made satellite, *Sputnik*, into space in 1957. The United

States worried that the Soviets might someday launch deadly missiles from outer space, and that shocking prospect set off a space race between the two rival superpowers. U.S. educators rushed to identify top students with scientific potential to help keep the country competitive in the technical battle. Talented girls, who had previously been ignored, now were urged to take advanced science courses for the nation's benefit.

Meanwhile, in the Deep South, the civil rights movement gained steam. A single act of defiance in Montgomery, Alabama, had grown into something

But one of the few women in the House of Representatives saw an unexpected opportunity.

momentous. In 1955, Rosa Parks refused to give up her bus seat to a white person and was arrested. The resulting bus boycott set in motion a long fight to win black Americans basic civil rights—the right to sit at any lunch counter, buy any home, and attend any school.

By the early 1960s blacks were marching and protesting to call attention to their plight, and their cries were heard. In 1964, Congress tackled one of the most groundbreaking laws of the era, the Civil Rights Act, intended to end racial discrimination in American life. A big piece of legislation like the Civil Rights Act is something like an elaborate quilt, with various patches representing different sections of the new law.

The Civil Rights Act of 1964 had several patches, or "titles." One focused on voting rights. Another ensured that restaurants, motels, and movie houses would be open to people of all races, and yet another barred discrimination in public schools. As the bill worked its way through the lawmaking process, legislators could propose amendments that changed or even eliminated the various sections. Only after all the amendments had been proposed and voted on, and all the remaining patches

pulled together, would the U.S. House of Representatives or the U.S. Senate vote on the entire bill. And both the House and the Senate would have to approve the bill before it could become law, making the whole process long and sometimes very frustrating.

One section of the Civil Rights Act, Title VII, was particularly thorny. This piece was intended to open all jobs to people of all races, and it created an Equal Employment Opportunity Commission (EEOC) to enforce the law. Many private businesses chafed at the government telling them who they should hire. Moreover, many southern congressmen, unwilling to give up a history of racial segregation, were strongly opposed to it.

The debate was long and heated, and when it looked like the section would pass the House of Representatives, Representative Howard W. Smith of Virginia stood up to make a daring amendment. Mr. Smith, a long-standing segregationist, proposed adding the word "sex" to the section, so that it would forbid job discrimination against women as well as blacks.

Mr. Smith's amendment was carefully calculated. He was strongly opposed to the bill, and he knew many

Opposite: U.S. Representatives Martha W. Griffiths *(far left),* Howard W. Smith *(center),* and Katharine St. George *(far right)* congratulate journalist May Craig *(second from left)* after the House agrees to include women in the 1964 Civil Rights Act banning job discrimination. Ms. Craig, a longtime journalist, had challenged Mr. Smith to include women on the *Meet the Press* television show.

14

southern legislators were against it too. He figured northern legislators who supported it might change their minds if the law required hiring women on an equal footing with men. Barring discrimination on the basis of sex just might convince a majority of legislators to reject the whole idea.

Mr. Smith proposed the change almost jokingly, saying that he was trying to help "the minority sex." The men on the House floor began chuckling and making jokes about the pro-posal. As the discussion progressed the guffaws grew louder.

But one of the few women in the House of Representatives saw an unexpected opportunity. Martha W. Griffiths, a representative from Michigan, knew the hilarity would have to stop if the proposal was going to have any chance at all. She rose to speak, beginning, "I presume that if there had been any necessity to point out that women were a second-class sex, the laughter would have proved it."

instant replay

Martha Wright Griffiths: Champion of Women's Rights

Martha Wright Griffiths grew up under the influence of strong women. Her grandmother sewed and managed a hotel to keep her three sons in school after her husband died. Her grandmother, a devoted suffragist, was first in line on the first Election Day after women won the right to vote.

Growing up in tiny Pierce City, Missouri, Martha was an eager student and a debater on the high school team. She was excited about going to college. But when hard times hit, her father concluded Martha would have to pass up college so that her brother could go. Martha's mother, however, wouldn't hear of it. She took in boarders, doubling her load of housework, so her daughter could attend the University of Missouri.

Determined to make the most of her college years, Martha became a zealous reader, consuming up to three books a weekend. She continued to debate, meeting her future husband, Hicks Griffiths, when they were paired on the debate team. After they married, Hicks turned down the chance to attend Harvard Law School because it didn't admit women. Instead, he and Martha attended the University of Michigan Law School together, finishing in 1940. Later, they would practice law together in Detroit, and when Martha decided to run for office, Hicks would become his wife's campaign manager, adviser, and biggest supporter.

Mrs. Griffiths was elected to the House of Representatives in 1954 and quickly became known for her sharp mind and equally sharp tongue.

She was best known for sponsoring the Equal Rights Amendment and making sure the Civil Rights Act of 1964 covered women. But she also helped change laws that denied women fair taxation, pensions, and military benefits.

She believed Congress had to address these issues because the Supreme Court for many years refused to apply the laws of the land to women. "My grandmother wanted to live long enough to vote for a woman president," she once said. "I'll be satisfied if I live to see a woman go before the Supreme Court and hear the justices acknowledge, 'Gentlemen, she's human. She deserves the protection of our laws.'"

Mrs. Griffiths, who died in 2003, got her wish.

Left: U.S. Representative Martha W. Griffiths of Michigan in front of the Capitol in 1970.

The men quickly quieted down.

Mrs. Griffiths argued passionately that women should be included in this section of the law. The members of the House listened carefully. And when the balloting time came, the House voted 168–133 to add "sex" to the hiring section of the Civil Rights Act.

A cheer came from the visitor's gallery. "We made it!" a woman cried out. "We are human!" And these new "humans" now would be able to compete for many more jobs.

Eventually, the Senate passed the bill too, with the provision for women intact. President Lyndon B. Johnson signed the Civil Rights Act into law on July 2, 1964, calling on the nation to "eliminate the last vestiges of injustice in America."

For girls coming of age in the 1960s, the debates in Congress seemed distant and almost irrelevant. They weren't discouraged from pursuing careers, but they weren't encouraged, either. In the frenzy over *Sputnik*, twelve-year-old Shirley Ann Jackson, an African American growing up in Washington, D.C., was selected for accelerated science and

Below: President Lyndon B. Johnson hands a pen to civil-rights leader Martin Luther King Jr. after signing the historic Civil Rights Act of 1964, banning race discrimination in many areas of American life. While the law also banned sex discrimination in the workplace, no women are visible at the signing.

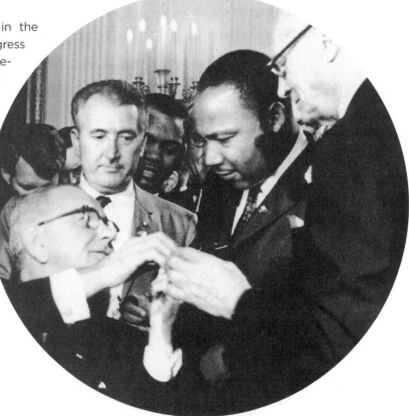

math classes starting in seventh grade. From an early age, she had collected bumblebees and yellow jackets and analyzed their diets and behavior. Studying biology, math, and physics seemed like a natural extension of her interests.

When the time came to apply for college in 1963, the assistant principal for boys, a black man, knew about her top grades and strong test scores and encouraged her to apply to the prestigious Massachusetts Institute of Technology (MIT). Shirley had never heard of MIT, but she applied and was admitted. The assistant principal for girls, a white woman, wasn't impressed. When Shirley's acceptance was announced to her homeroom, this assistant principal told the class that the young woman was "trying to be too big for her britches" by going to MIT instead of a black college.

At MIT, with just a few dozen women and only five African Americans in a freshman class of one thousand, many students initially shunned Shirley. Some professors doubted women or blacks were capable of the work. One professor went so far as to tell Shirley that "colored girls should learn a trade." Shirley was determined not to be discouraged. "I picked a trade," she said. "I picked physics."

She became the first African-American woman to receive a Ph.D. from MIT, earning hers in theoretical particle physics in 1973. In the 1990s she became chair of the Nuclear Regulatory Commission and, later, president of Rensselaer Polytechnic Institute, a top technology school.

Like Shirley Jackson, Susan Love was invited to participate in special summer science programs after *Sputnik* and was one of a small group of students in advanced classes in her school in the mid-1960s. But while counselors encouraged the boys to apply to Harvard and MIT, the girls didn't get any specific college counseling at all. "It never occurred to me that I could apply to any of those places," she said.

She attended Fordham University and studied chemistry, hoping to become a doctor. When the time came to apply, she carefully chose which medical schools to send her applications to. Most medical schools at the time made clear that they would accept only a few women each year, stopping when the quota was filled. Even her premed adviser tried

Opposite: U.S. Representatives Charlotte Reid, Patsy Mink, and Catherine May protest their exclusion from the congressional gym because they are female, though they are also members of Congress.

"We made it!" a woman cried out. *"We are human!"*

instant replay

For Members Only

The few women elected to Congress in the 1960s had most of the same privileges as the men did, except one: They couldn't use the congressional swimming pool and gym. The sign said MEMBERS ONLY, but women members were not welcome.

Three representatives—Charlotte Reid of Illinois, Patsy Mink of Hawaii, and Catherine May of Washington—saw the closed door as just another way in which women were shut out by social customs and old habits. Congressmen could talk out issues or make deals in the gym, but the women couldn't join in.

In protest, the three tried to enter one day in 1967, but they were turned away. The reason? The men liked to swim in the nude, they were told.

"So," recalled Mrs. Mink, "we said, 'Is it too much for the democratic process to ask you to put your pants on?'"

Apparently so. Congresswomen were given access to the pool, but only in the early-morning hours, when the men didn't want to swim.

MEMBERS ONLY

to talk her out of applying. When she asked him for the required letter of recommendation, he told her she should become a biochemistry teacher. At the time, men who went to graduate school could defer being drafted for the Vietnam War. If Susan went to medical school, the adviser told her, she "would kill some boy." She would be taking a man's spot, presumably sending him off to war.

She applied anyway, earning her medical degree from the State University of New York. She went on to become a surgeon and one of the nation's most prominent advocates for breast cancer research and education.

In the mid-1960s surgery and particle physics seemed like far-fetched choices for most females. Most married women had their hands full taking care of their families. In the days before disposable diapers, wrinkle-free fabrics, fast food, and microwave ovens, much of their time was spent cooking meals, washing and ironing their families' clothing, and taking care of children.

Still, roughly two of every five women worked, often as secretaries, retail clerks, nurses, teachers, or librarians. Many women ran into discrimination at work, where they were pushed into the lowest-paying jobs, denied promotions, or refused the chance to apply for better jobs. By 1966 women had filed more than four thousand complaints with the new Equal Employment Opportunity Commission. At the time, however, the commission wasn't interested. Including women in the law had been a "fluke," a top official for the commission told one gathering, as if that was a reason why the law didn't need to be enforced.

The cavalier attitude angered women who had been fighting so hard for a fair shake. In reaction, a group of women that year hastily formed the National Organization for Women, or NOW, at a conference on women. NOW's goal would be to push for better enforcement of the law and to seek "full equality for women." The group chose as its leader Betty Friedan, whose best-selling 1963 book, *The Feminine Mystique*, had awakened millions of women to the possibility that their lives could be more than housework.

The creation of NOW infused the women's rights movement with a new energy. With it, the seeds of the second wave of the women's movement took root and began to grow.

Including women in the law had been a "fluke" . . .

instant replay

Libbers and Bra Burners

In social movements, high-profile or even outrageous acts sometimes help bring attention to a cause and crystallize the issues.

To some women, the Miss America pageant seemed to symbolize the nation's irrational emphasis on a woman's beauty and body shape over brains and skills. In 1968 about one hundred demonstrators gathered in Atlantic City, New Jersey, to call attention to what they called "ludicrous beauty standards." (A separate group, protesting racism in the Miss America contest, held a competing Miss Black America pageant a few blocks away.)

The protestors, carrying signs and a swimsuit-clad puppet, said they were part of the women's liberation movement. They paraded around a crowned sheep, since women were being judged like livestock at a show. And they dropped hair curlers, high heels, false eyelashes, girdles, and bras into a "freedom trash can" to symbolize the "enslavement" of women.

The mayor of Atlantic City had worried that something would be burned, in the way men were burning draft cards in protest of the Vietnam War. In a meeting "we told him we wouldn't do anything dangerous— just a symbolic bra-burning," said one organizer.

The women kept their promise. There was no fire. But after the protest got national attention, those who were outspoken about women's rights were often dismissed as "women's libbers" or "bra burners."

Above:

A protestor drops a bra into a trash barrel outside the 1968 Miss America Pageant.

Above: On August 26, 1970, fifty years after women won the right to vote, more than fifty thousand people marched down Fifth Avenue in New York City, seeking equality for women at work and at home.

Soon, every state in the nation had groups that encouraged women to stand up for their rights. They pushed elected officials to acknowledge the value of women's work in the home, at school, and at the office. As the 1970s approached, a growing number of Americans were ready to see women fully participate in society for the first time in U.S. history.

A growing number of Americans were ready to see women fully participate in society for the first time.

chapter 3
pregame preparation

"During my lifetime, I would only have liked equal treatment, equal opportunity."
—Edith Green, U.S. representative, in many speeches

In the 1960s, U.S. Representative Edith Starrett Green worked hard to provide equal opportunities for girls and boys. As a congresswoman from Portland, Oregon, she promoted laws that funded new colleges so that more students could attend. She helped to create the first federal scholarships and loans so that all students who wanted to go to college could go, regardless of their ability to pay. The small, graying former teacher was passionate about making education available to everyone.

So she was shocked at what she heard one day in the late 1960s, several years after the passage of the Civil Rights Act. A panel of school superintendents spoke at a hearing about a special program for potential high school dropouts.

One superintendent boasted that his state was having great success with its new program for disadvan-

taged boys. Many more of them were staying in school. Two other superintendents chimed in that their new classes for boys were a hit as well.

Mrs. Green thought she misunderstood the men. "Did you choose your words carefully? Do you mean that you had classes only for disadvantaged boys?" she quizzed them.

"Yes," they answered.

"Well, was there not a need to have classes for disadvantaged girls?" she asked. She knew for a fact that many girls dropped out of high school too. "Couldn't you have classes and include both boys and girls?" she wondered.

Oh, no, the superintendents said; it was better to have classes just for boys. The boys needed them, they explained, because they "are going to have to be the breadwinners."

Mrs. Green was stunned. How could school leaders believe education was more important for boys than for girls? More girls and women were working to provide for themselves and their families than at any other time in American history. In fact, eight out of every ten girls in school at the

"It was perfectly legal to discriminate in any education program against girls or women," she found.

time would be employed at some point in their lives. Without an education, they would have a tough time getting decent jobs at decent pay.

Certainly, she thought, the laws of the United States didn't allow this kind of discrimination. Certainly, the nation's laws wouldn't let public schools give boys opportunities that they didn't give to girls. But when she looked up the laws in place, she learned that schools were indeed free to offer more and better programs to boys than to girls. "It was perfectly legal to discriminate in any education program against girls or women," she found.

To Edith Green, that was simply unacceptable. The superintendents' comments, she said later, "made me determined that I was going to change the law so that they could no longer discriminate."

But changing the laws of the United States of America isn't quick or easy. As a U.S. representative, Mrs. Green had to come up with facts and evidence that spelled out why a law was needed. She wanted to have the support of a U.S. House of Representatives' committee that specialized in education. She would then have to

win the support of at least half of the 435 members of the House.

Meanwhile, the same idea would need the backing of at least a majority of the one hundred members of the U.S. Senate, a separate governing body that also proposed laws. (In the Senate, sometimes a bill needs even more than majority support. A few members can "filibuster" a bill in the Senate, a fancy term for talking endlessly to delay a vote. In that case, sixty votes are needed to end the debate and get on with business.)

Both the House and the Senate—together comprising the Congress—had to agree before a proposal could become a law. Then the president of the United States needed to sign the law to make it official.

It could have been a very daunting prospect—but Edith Green wasn't easily discouraged. She knew firsthand how disappointing and frustrating discrimination could be. Born in 1910 as the middle of five children, she had excelled in high school as a student, tennis player, and debater, winning a statewide award as Oregon's "Outstanding Girl." Her classmates elected her valedictorian her senior year, the first girl to win that honor at her Salem, Oregon, school.

In high school she decided she wanted to be a lawyer. But her parents and a favorite teacher told her straight out that a woman lawyer wasn't likely to actually try cases. Instead, she "would undoubtedly be in the back room doing research or drawing up briefs." They urged her to consider teaching or nursing instead, the only respectable professions for a young lady.

She worked at a cannery to help pay her way through Willamette University, but her money ran out. She turned to a less ambitious program at a nearby teacher's college, where it took her only one year to earn a teaching certificate. She taught sixth grade and junior high for many years, beginning in 1930. While continuing to teach, she married in 1933 and finally earned her college degree in 1939. Though she had loved teaching, she never forgot that as a girl, she had to put her dreams aside.

Left: U.S. Representative Edith Green of Oregon in her congressional office in 1969.

As a teacher and a mother of two sons, she became active in the Parent-Teacher Association, starting down a road that led her into state and then national politics. Elected to the U.S. Congress in 1954, she made her mark on school issues over many years, earning the nickname "Mrs. Education."

Like Martha Griffiths, she was part of the first wave of women elected to Congress on their own, rather than to fill their husbands' seats, and she wasn't always warmly received. Many men in Congress teased their female colleagues, dismissed their ideas, or ignored them altogether. Mrs. Green had no patience for that and let them know it. With what one reporter called an "unladylike aptitude for hard political infighting," she could be very tough on her political opponents, sometimes refusing to speak to them for months. "She's a bare-knuckle fighter who's capable of really whiplashing her opponents," one Washington insider said.

Some fellow representatives were afraid of her. Some genuinely disliked her. And privately, some had another nickname for Mrs. Green: They called her "the wicked witch of the West."

Even her supporters found her prickly at times. Though she was a

instant replay

The Equal Pay Act

On the surface, politics is the business of leading governments. But as newly elected officials quickly learn, politics is really about negotiation. Edith Green got a long lesson in that skill after she proposed the Equal Pay Act as a freshman congresswoman in May 1955.

The act called for employers to pay women and men the same wages for the same work. That was a radical idea in the 1950s, when women's work was automatically considered inferior to men's. Nationwide working women earned just fifty-nine cents for every dollar that working men earned.

Mrs. Green's bill was sent to the House Education and Labor Committee, whose purpose was to study and approve education and work-related bills before the whole House would vote on them. Because so many laws are proposed each year, the committee didn't have time to consider every single one. Many simply were ignored.

Mrs. Green feared that's what would happen to her bill. Every time she suggested that hearings be held on the issue, she said, her fellow committee members "were struck with instant deafness."

She began to press harder. While campaigning for John F. Kennedy in 1959 and 1960, Mrs. Green lobbied him until she won his support. She also tried shrewd tactics. One day she sat down behind a key committee member from Georgia in the House of Representatives. Would he do her a favor? she asked. With southern charm, he responded, "Anything, Edith, anything."

"Well," Mrs. Green said, beginning to pull his leg, "I have a little old bill that I want to introduce and when I tell you about it, you can understand why I'm reluctant to do it. But you could do it."

With a straight face, she explained that male members of Congress "have a great deal more work than women members of Congress." The men do more research and work longer hours, she went on. So, she said, maybe a bill should be proposed that called for paying male members of Congress more than female members.

The congressman sputtered with outrage. He wouldn't introduce any such legislation. "You know that you women have to work harder than men do," he told her.

"I'm so glad to hear you say that," Mrs. Green responded. And then she reminded him that her "little old bill" calling for equal pay for the same work had been languishing before his committee for years. Couldn't they get to work on it?

He got the message. The committee finally did consider the bill, but many members just didn't believe women should be paid the same as men in every job. Ultimately, Mrs. Green had to agree to a major concession. The bill would apply to workers who were paid by the hour, like factory workers and janitors. But salaried jobs would be excluded. Women managers and lawyers, teachers and school principals would not be guaranteed the same pay as men doing exactly the same work.

Congress passed the Equal Pay Act in 1963—eight years after Mrs. Green first introduced it. Despite its shortcomings, it was a significant equal rights law for women. And though it applied to just one in three working women, it had a major impact. In the following years millions of dollars in back pay would be awarded to hundreds of thousands of workers who had been paid less just because they were female.

huge fan of President John F. Kennedy in the early 1960s, she didn't hesitate to criticize his administration if she thought its proposals were ill conceived. That frustrated some in his administration. Maybe, they figured, they would get more help from Mrs. Green "if we treated her like a woman." Some of them "wined and dined her" to try to make her more cooperative.

But she knew why she had been elected to Congress and stuck to what she thought was right. Even after being wined and dined, Mrs. Green didn't budge. "When she disagreed with us on a point of substance, I never saw her give an inch," one government official told *The Wall Street Journal* in 1969.

Despite her demanding and strong-willed demeanor, she was also known as an incredibly hard worker who always did her homework. Her speeches were so thoughtful and

Right: A reelection brochure for Mrs. Green's 1962 campaign promotes her ties to President Kennedy.

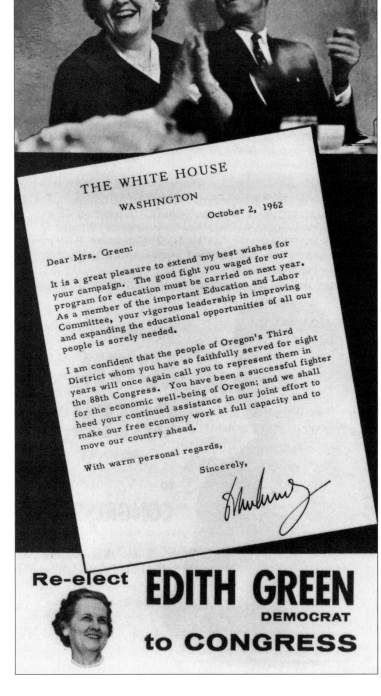

THE WHITE HOUSE
WASHINGTON

October 2, 1962

Dear Mrs. Green:

It is a great pleasure to extend my best wishes for your campaign. The good fight you waged for our program for education must be carried on next year. As a member of the important Education and Labor Committee, your vigorous leadership in improving and expanding the educational opportunities of all our people is sorely needed.

I am confident that the people of Oregon's Third District whom you have so faithfully served for eight years will once again call you to represent them in the 88th Congress. You have been a successful fighter for the economic well-being of Oregon; and we shall heed your continued assistance in our joint effort to make our free economy work at full capacity and to move our country ahead.

With warm personal regards,

Sincerely,

Re-elect **EDITH GREEN** DEMOCRAT **to CONGRESS**

convincing that the usually noisy House members quieted down to listen to her. She could be so persuasive that other representatives would change their votes on the spot, making her a formidable opponent in a debate.

After that eye-opening day when the superintendents spoke about special classes for boys only, she put her energy behind a law that would give girls the same opportunities as boys in school. Many congressmen opposed such a radical step. Girls, they believed, simply didn't need the same education or opportunities as boys, and they shouldn't take spots that might otherwise go to males.

Even her supporters knew this was a major—and risky—undertaking. To have a chance at seeing this law passed, Mrs. Green would have to be clever and be ready to compromise. Only a very skilled politician could make it happen, one political aide said at the time. "But if anyone can get it passed," the aide added, "Mrs. Green's probably the one."

chapter 4
opening
kickoff

"Placing limits on the intellectual aspirations of women should be alien to the very basic concepts of this nation."
—Edith Green, 1971

As 1970 approached, Mrs. Green remembered the school superintendents and their boys-only programs, and she found herself in a good position to do something about them. She had been in Congress for nearly fifteen years and had climbed the political ranks of the House Education and Labor Committee. She was now the chairwoman of one of its three subcommittees, the one specializing in higher education. This influential job gave her the power to help choose what laws the committee would actually consider.

The challenge would be convincing others that the law had to change.

A congressional aide urged Mrs. Green to hold hearings on how girls and women were faring in education to help Congress and the public better understand the problems. But congressional hearings required experts to testify. There were few studies or books or commissions on how females were treated at school. Who would come?

Bernice Resnick Sandler had the answer. The woman everyone called "Bunny" had earned her doctorate in educational counseling at the University of Maryland in 1969, and like Mrs. Green, she had some sharp words resounding in her head. She had applied for teaching jobs at her university, but her department didn't consider her for any of its seven job openings. When she asked a colleague why, he was blunt.

"Let's face it," he said. "You come on too strong for a woman."

Too strong? Dr. Sandler was sure she had done something wrong. But she came to realize that employers didn't want women to be too strong— or too educated. Despite her credentials, an employment counselor

Above: Bernice Resnick "Bunny" Sandler speaks at a 1971 women's meeting.

29

The comic strip panels contain the following dialogue:

Panel 1: "B.U. LAW SCHOOL? WELL, OPEN IT UP!" "WHY? WHAT'S THE POINT? I ALREADY KNOW WHAT IT SAYS.."

Panel 2: "GIVE IT HERE, KIDDO!" "IT'S A REJECTION. I'M QUITE SURE OF THAT. I'VE NEVER BEEN MORE SURE OF ANYTHING IN MY LIFE."

Panel 3: "IT'S BECAUSE I'M A WOMAN— THAT'S WHY, YOU KNOW. ABSOLUTELY. IT'S BECAUSE I'M A MIDDLE-AGED WOMAN, AND NO LAW SCHOOL IS GOING TO BELIEVE IN ME. I KNOW IT."

Panel 4: "DEAR SIR..." "I KNEW IT!"

told her she wasn't a professional, "just a housewife who went back to school." Another potential employer told her he didn't hire women because they stayed home when their children were sick.

Their behavior seemed immoral, Dr. Sandler reasoned, "so it must be illegal." But like Mrs. Green, she, too, discovered that schools weren't breaking any laws when they turned down women just for being women.

Angry and frustrated, she began to collect information about how women graduate students and faculty members were treated at the University of Maryland. Her research led her to other women who shared similar experiences at universities around the country. While many universities had many tuition-paying female students, she found, many hired women only for the lowest-level teaching jobs. In fact, some schools hadn't hired a female professor in decades.

Dr. Sandler filed complaints against more than two hundred universities with the federal government and compiled her findings into a report. She printed two hundred copies and sent some to select members of Congress, including Mrs. Green. With the help of Dr. Sandler, her complaints and her "horror stories," Mrs. Green now had facts and figures and a list of people who could tell Congress about all kinds of discrimination against women in education.

Hearings were held in June and July 1970, and the experience was chilling—in more ways than one. The air-conditioning was working on overdrive, making the meeting room uncomfortable. The testimony made listeners even more uncomfortable. Over seven days distinguished women, scholars, and government officials outlined the many ways women were shut out of opportunities:

- State universities in Virginia had turned away 21,000 women in the early 1960s; during the same time period not a single man was turned away.
- A brochure from the University of North Carolina declared that admission of women—but not men—

was "restricted to those who are especially well-qualified." As a result, the 1970 freshman class had nearly 1,900 men and only 426 women.

- At the University of Michigan more qualified female students applied than male students. So the school "adjusted" its requirements to keep girls to less than half of the freshman class. Officials didn't want an "over-balance" of females.
- Quotas at many medical and law schools limited females to just five or ten students out of every one hundred. Consequently, just 7 percent of the doctors in the United States at the end of the 1960s were women.
- Even though most teachers from grade school through high school were women, they were rarely promoted. Most principals were men.

Though Mrs. Green found the facts astonishing, few other people heard them. No newspapers covered the testimony. And while Mrs. Green ran the hearings every day, no more than four of the fifteen male congressmen on the subcommittee ever showed up at one time.

instant replay

Cross-Country in Connecticut

As girls and young women began to demand more options in school and outside, they often ran into resistance from adults who believed girls and boys should stick to traditional roles.

As a sophomore, Susan Hollander wanted to run cross-country and track for Hamden High School. She was talented enough to make the boys' team, and the coach was willing to have her. But she was turned away because the Connecticut Interscholastic Athletic Conference prohibited girls and boys from competing together.

She sued to challenge the league's rule in a New Haven state court. In March 1971, Judge John Clark FitzGerald sided with the athletic league, agreeing that boys and girls shouldn't be on the same team. He wrote, "The present generation of our younger male population has not become so decadent that boys will experience a thrill in defeating girls in running contests, whether the girls be members of their own team or of an adversary team."

He continued: "Athletic competition builds character in our boys. We do not need that kind of character in our girls, the women of tomorrow."

Susan and her lawyers pursued their legal challenge, and the next year the association changed its rules and allowed her to run. Her experience wouldn't be forgotten, however. The judge's words would be quoted again and again as an example of the entrenched attitudes girls had to overcome.

Determined that others should hear about the injustices women were facing, Mrs. Green hired Dr. Sandler to put together the written record of the hearings. Dr. Sandler compiled the statements, testimony, and reports into two fat books, figuring that heft would make the issue seem more important. Though the government usually prints just a few hundred copies of most hearings, Mrs. Green had six thousand copies printed. To help get the word out, she personally sent a note and a copy to all 535 members of Congress.

But despite the evidence she had collected, Mrs. Green's male colleagues simply weren't interested in changing the law in 1970.

Since representatives are elected every two years, 1971 brought in a new crop of legislators. This time, Mrs. Green tried to sneak in a new law.

Both the House and the Senate would be discussing a major education bill to replace an old law that was expiring. In the elaborate process of becoming the law of the land, this bill had a long and treacherous trip ahead. Once both the House and the Senate each had a version, a few members from each would huddle in a conference committee to iron out differences between the two bills. A single

bill would go back to both the House and the Senate for final approval. Only then would the bill go to President Richard Nixon for his signature.

If this bill, which became known as the Education Amendments of 1972, was a giant quilt, most of the patches would contain detailed proposals for new financial aid for colleges and college students. In addition, President Nixon's administration wanted this education bill to include a provision limiting school busing. At the time more and more courts were ordering school districts to racially integrate by busing black students to traditionally white schools and white students to traditionally black schools. Such court-ordered busing was controversial and was causing uproar in many communities. That subject, too, took up several patches of the quilt.

As the higher-education expert in the House, Mrs. Green had worked on virtually every piece of the quilt for more than a year and was a main sponsor and author of the House version. She knew she also wanted this big education bill to outlaw discrimination against women and girls in schools. But she didn't want that tiny piece of the bill to be too prominent.

"I stand on the shoulders of these *brave people*."

player profile

Ruth Bader Ginsburg, U.S. Supreme Court Justice

Ruth Bader Ginsburg became a lawyer in the late 1950s, but her legal career really took off in the 1970s, when she began challenging how American laws viewed women.

As a law student, she was one of just a few women in her class. Admissions quotas discouraged women from trying law school, as did the prospects after graduation. "It was the sense that, well, I can go through three years of law school and then what?" she said. "Who will hire me and how will I support myself?"

Though she graduated at the top of her class at Columbia Law School, not a single New York law firm would hire her. Eventually, she taught at a law school. As the women's movement gained steam she began to work with the American Civil Liberties Union on women's rights cases.

Between 1972 and 1978, Ms. Ginsburg argued six cases before the U.S. Supreme Court and won five of them, greatly expanding constitutional rights for women. Sometimes the discrimination was against a man. In one case, a father wanted to collect Social Security benefits after his wife died so he could stay home with his infant son. A widow would have received the benefits. But the system assumed that men worked and women stayed home. The Supreme Court agreed that the law was unconstitutional.

Appointed a federal appeals court judge in 1980, Judge Ginsburg was named to the U.S. Supreme Court in 1993. At her confirmation hearings she gave credit to those who had toiled to end slavery and win the vote for women. "I surely would not be in this room today without the determined efforts of men and women who kept dreams alive, dreams of equal citizenship in the days when few would listen," she said. "I stand on the shoulders of these brave people."

Left: Ruth Bader Ginsburg is sworn in as a member of the United States Supreme Court in 1993.

Cleverly, she waited to even mention outlawing sex discrimination in schools until the bill was before the entire House Education and Labor Committee. There, she had key supporters, including Shirley Chisholm of New York, the first African-American congresswoman, and Patsy Mink of Hawaii, the first woman of color elected to Congress, who helped write the section that would apply to girls and women.

When the full committee was gathered, Mrs. Green proposed adding a little section to the education bill that would ban sex discrimination in programs and activities at any school that received federal money. If schools treated girls or boys unfairly or denied girls admission because they were female—or if school superintendents continued to offer special programs for boys and not for girls— the schools could lose their federal money. That was a huge penalty, considering the federal government might pay for everything from school lunches to college tuition to university research.

When Mrs. Green finally introduced this idea, the meeting room was packed. Some committee members thought such a change was unnecessary, even silly. One male representative made fun of the idea, saying that it might have the unintended result of men doing women's work. At the time only young women known as stewardesses served drinks and food on airlines. "If this passes," he said, "you are going to have male stewards." The room erupted in laughter at the preposterous notion.

But despite the upsetting possibility that men might someday parcel out peanuts to travelers, a majority of the thirty-five committee members approved Mrs. Green's suggestion. This new section was like a tassel or, at most, a small square on the bigger quilt. Originally called Title X, the section later became Title IX after another piece of the bill was dropped.

The next battleground was the House of Representatives.

Mrs. Green figured that with so many hot-button issues on the table, the little piece requiring fair play for both sexes might be largely overlooked. At one point as the bill progressed Dr. Sandler, who worked for the Women's Equity Action League, and other women's rights supporters wanted to help support Title IX by calling and visiting legislators. But Mrs. Green told them to be low key. "Nobody knows what's in this bill," the congresswoman told them. "If you start asking questions, lobbying for it, they're going to ask questions."

Mrs. Green's instincts were right. The House stayed focused on the financial aid and busing sections of the bill and debated for days and days on those sections. Still, when Mrs. Green's proposal was noticed, it was a touchy topic. Both the *New York Times* and the *Washington Post* argued against it. Though "motivated by the best of intentions," the *Times* said, "such legislation is educationally unsound" because men and women have different needs and aspirations.

House members had strong feelings on both sides. When the proposal came up for debate on the House floor on November 4, 1971, John N. Erlenborn, a representative

Think of her as your mother.

She only wants what's best for you.
A cool drink. A good dinner.
A soft pillow and a warm blanket.
This is not just maternal instinct. It's the result
of the longest Stewardess training in the industry.
Training in service, not just a beauty course.
Service, after all, is what makes professional travellers
prefer American.
And makes new travellers want to keep on flying with us.
So we see that every passenger gets
the same professional treatment.
That's the American Way.

Fly the American Way
American Airlines

from Illinois, was sharply critical. Of course, he told his House colleagues, he wasn't opposed to women attending college. But he had heard from some of the nation's most prominent universities, and they didn't want the U.S. government telling them how many women they should admit.

The proposal was "a dangerous precedent," he warned. "I feel that if

Above: An American Airlines ad from the late 1960s played up the nurturing role of its all-female flight attendants, then known as "stewardesses."

House members had
strong feelings on both sides.

Congress permits the Federal Government to take away from colleges their right to determine the composition of their own student bodies, it will plant the seed of destruction for our system of higher education as we know it."

In a letter to Mr. Erlenborn, Harvard University made it clear that it wasn't ready to consider applicants to its all-female Radcliffe College on an equal footing with applicants to its all-male Harvard College. But the school was considering a smaller change, admitting 450 women, up from 300, while trimming the number of men to 1,150 from 1,175.

If Congress required the university to consider men and women based solely on their qualifications, Harvard would suffer, it said. If it increased the size of its student body, it would be short of housing and teachers. Conversely, if it admitted fewer men and more women, it would face "educational and financial risks of a different kind."

That's because, Harvard said, male alumni gave far more money to the school than female graduates did, and the school needed their financial support. In addition, since women were less inclined to study science, a larger female student body might overwhelm the already-crowded humanities and social sciences departments. (Actually, that wasn't totally true, the student newspaper, the *Harvard Crimson*, reported. According to admissions officials, Radcliffe freshmen were more interested in studying science than Harvard freshmen.)

Harvard wasn't the only university that was worried. Yale, Princeton, and Notre Dame universities, among others, also contacted lawmakers to warn of the calamities, financial and otherwise, that might befall them if they had to admit more women or consider female applicants on the same basis as males.

Mr. Erlenborn saw their logic and asked the House to make a change. The new law, he said, shouldn't apply at all to undergraduate admissions. The law could still require graduate schools, such as law schools and medical schools, to consider women equally with men. It would still outlaw sex discrimination in hiring and pay at schools and universities. But he would protect a university's right to reject female undergraduates because of their sex rather than their abilities.

Many representatives agreed with him that Title IX would force schools to accept fixed numbers of males and

player profile

Patsy Takemoto Mink, the First Woman of Color in Congress

Patsy Takemoto Mink ran into plenty of barriers because she was female. But she didn't pay much attention to girls' issues until her daughter was growing up.

As a child of Japanese immigrants in Hawaii, she was far more sensitive to racial issues. After America entered World War II, some Japanese Americans were jailed for fear they would join with the enemy. Others, including her father, were harassed.

From the time she was little, Patsy wanted to become a doctor. But even though she was a gifted student, she was rejected from more than a dozen medical schools because they accepted few, if any, women and few people of color.

A mentor encouraged her to consider other options. "Why don't you go to law school?" she said. "You like to talk." Mrs. Mink took her advice and got a law degree from the University of Chicago. But again, she hit a wall: No one would hire her.

She returned to Hawaii with her husband and their infant daughter, Gwendolyn, whom she called Wendy, and opened her own law practice. She became involved in Hawaii politics and was elected to Congress in 1964.

As her daughter grew, Mrs. Mink became concerned about how girls were treated at school. One year, for instance, Wendy's classmates elected her the class president. But Wendy's teacher made her the vice president instead, telling her that only boys should be president.

If anything convinced Mrs. Mink to work for laws that required schools to give girls the same opportunities as boys, she said, "it was the experiences that my daughter kept bringing home to me from elementary school, intermediate school, and high school."

females, with the government dictating the student mix.

Edith Green insisted that wasn't true. In fact, she opposed any kind of quotas, or fixed goals. "All I want and all I ask," she said, "is that if two individuals, a man and a woman, come to a college or university and they have equal credentials and apply for admissions, that they shall be treated as equals."

Patsy Mink, too, was indignant. Two years before, her daughter Wendy had been turned down by Stanford University, which told applicants straight out that 40 percent of its students would be women and 60 percent would be men, no matter what their grades or qualifications were. At the time Wendy thought that she simply wasn't good enough to get in. But her mother knew her daughter was a top-notch student

Above: U.S. Representative Patsy Mink of Hawaii in 1972.

and was furious that a quota—not her skills—might have kept her out.

"Millions of women pay taxes into the Federal treasury and we collectively resent that these funds should be used for the support of institutions to which we are denied equal access," Mrs. Mink argued, urging House members to oppose Mr. Erlenborn's change. Without a fair shot at the same undergraduate schools, she said, women couldn't possibly compete with men for graduate schools or good jobs after college.

Men spoke in support of Title IX as well. Ed Koch, a representative from New York, criticized his fellow lawmakers for trying to dole out rights to women in "dribs and drabs" rather than granting them full opportunities. These were "salami tactics," he said, "that is to say, 'rights, a slice at a time.'"

But when the vote was taken, Mr. Erlenborn's change was approved—by just five votes.

The debate on the other sections of the education bill would stretch deep into the night. In the early hours of the next day the House approved the entire education bill—financial aid, busing restrictions, and a toned-down Title IX altogether.

Later, a congressman from Ohio would tell Mrs. Green that he voted

for the Erlenborn change because it was necessary. "If there are a limited number of places in colleges," he said, "men are going to be the breadwinners and they should be given preference." It was the same old story.

The *Washington Post* called the Erlenborn vote a setback for the female House members. Bella Abzug, an outspoken congresswoman from New York, called it "utterly shameful." Mrs. Mink called the outcome a "day of catastrophe."

Only Edith Green, the political veteran, saw the situation differently. She had her eye on the big picture, knowing that politicians rarely get everything they want. Yes, Title IX was important, but even with the change, women would now have a fair shot at graduate schools. Who could have imagined then that women would

storm law schools and medical schools once they were given the chance?

In contrast to Title IX, the financial-aid portion of Mrs. Green's bill seemed much broader and more important. It would affect all students—male and female—allowing more low-income and middle-class children the opportunity to get a college degree than ever before. Nearly all of the points in her financial-aid package had made it through the intense and rigorous debate intact, and the only major concession in the whole bill was Mr. Erlenborn's change to Title IX.

For that, Mrs. Green was truly grateful. "I was really in seventh heaven," she said later. "I don't know when I have ever been so pleased, because I had worked so long, and it had been such a tough battle."

chapter 5
political football

> "No person in the United States shall, on the basis of sex, be excluded from participation in, be denied the benefits of, or be subjected to discrimination under any educational program or activity receiving Federal financial assistance."
>
> —The beginning of Title IX, 1972

Right: U.S. Senator Birch Bayh of Indiana in 1972.

While Edith Green was fighting to get her education bill and Title IX through the House of Representatives, a similar battle was under way in the United States Senate. There, it met a very different response.

As the entire Senate discussed its own education bill in August 1971, Birch Bayh, a senator from Indiana, introduced a proposal to bar sex discrimination in schools. He was drawing in part on a recommendation from a women's task force appointed by President Nixon, and the proposal seemed to have plenty of support. Mr.

41

scorecard 1971–72

High school	Boys	Girls
Total participating in varsity sports	3,666,917	294,015
Playing:		
Football (boys)/Volleyball (girls)	932,691	17,952
Basketball	645,670	132,299
Baseball/Softball	400,906	9,813
Soccer	78,510	700
Track and field	642,639	62,211

College	Men	Women
Playing in sports	170,384	29,977
Bachelor's degrees awarded	500,590	386,683
Students entering medical schools	10,435	1,653
Students in law schools	85,554	8,914
Students in veterinary schools	5,158	702

Bayh was confident it would pass. He reminded his fellow senators that quotas in place were keeping women from pursuing their dreams, and he encouraged them to take up the cause. "If Congress is to solve this knotty problem, if the benefits of a free and open society are to be extended to all Americans, now is the time to act," he told them.

Another senator quizzed Mr. Bayh about how universities would be affected, peppering him with questions about how the law would work. The questioning may have been planned in advance to be a colloquy, or dialogue—a method lawmakers use to spell out exactly what they have in mind for the legislative record. That way, even many years later, courts, regulators, and citizens would understand their thinking.

And in this question-and-answer dialogue, for the only time in the entire debate, the subject of sports came up.

Until then, lawmakers hadn't considered the issue of girls, schools, and sports. But girls and women who loved to run or shoot baskets or swing a bat were very aware that few schools offered competitive sports for them. In 1971 basketball was the most common sport for both sexes, with high schools sponsoring nearly twenty thousand boys' basketball teams and just five thousand girls' teams. Nearly thirteen thousand high schools had boys' baseball teams, but fewer than four hundred schools sponsored a girls' softball team. Many girls with athletic talent were simply shut out.

The June 1970 *Swimming World* magazine reported that the Norfolk Sports Club of Norfolk, Virginia, had named Steve Whitney the "Outstanding High School Swimmer." But he wasn't the fastest swimmer in the area or even at his school. That was Joanne Washcalus, who had set five records at an Amateur Athletic Union meet. Since their school didn't have a girls' swim team and the high school league didn't let girls compete with boys, Joanne's achievements were simply ignored.

Athletic girls were so frustrated by the lack of opportunities that more and more of them were demanding a chance to play baseball or tennis or run track with the boys. That unsettled many coaches and school officials. But what really made them uncomfortable was the thought that girls might try to join the most popular of boys' sports: football.

In his questioning of Mr. Bayh, Peter Dominick, senator from Colorado, asked how Mr. Bayh's proposal would mix boys and girls. Would men and women share dormitories? And would they have to share athletic facilities and equipment?

player profile

Birch Bayh, Advocate for Equal Rights

In his eighteen years in the Senate, Birch Bayh was a staunch supporter of women's rights, introducing not only Title IX in the Senate, but also the Equal Rights Amendment. The influence for his political positions came from both the women and the men in his family, as well as deeply held beliefs about how people should be treated.

Growing up in Indiana in the 1930s and '40s, he saw his grandmother work hard on the family farm and take an active role in business decisions. His first wife, who died of cancer, taught him lessons early on about discrimination. An A student in high school and a talented debater, she had wanted to attend the University of Virginia but was told women shouldn't bother to apply.

His father, a longtime educator, also had strong views. Once, when Mr. Bayh was about eleven years old, his father announced at breakfast that he would be testifying before Congress that day. As the director of physical education for a school district, his father planned to tell lawmakers that they needed to make money available for physical education for girls as well as for boys.

The money was important, his dad told him, because "little girls need strong bodies to carry their minds around just like little boys do."

Mr. Bayh remembered his father's words when Title IX became a law and, later, when the debate turned to sports. Though he left the Senate in 1981, he has remained a tireless advocate for Title IX and for the need of both boys and girls to have strong bodies and strong minds.

'I don't know what you chicks are complaining about. We're just trying to protect your feminine mystique.'

Above: A Bill Sanders editorial cartoon in the *Milwaukee Journal* in 1970.

Right: U.S. Senator Strom Thurmond of South Carolina in 1970.

Mr. Bayh was clear in his answer. "I do not read this as requiring integration of dormitories between the sexes, nor do I feel it mandates the desegregation of football fields," he replied. "What we are trying to do is provide equal access for women and men students to the educational process and the extracurricular activities in a school." Nothing in the law, he insisted, would call for women to play football with men or to share the men's locker room.

"If I may say so," Mr. Dominick replied, "I would have had much more fun playing college football if it had been integrated."

"The Senator from Indiana will resist the temptation to remark further on that point," Mr. Bayh responded.

The men in the Senate laughed, and the talk about sports ended.

Before long, the debate turned more serious. Senator Strom Thurmond of South Carolina asked if The Citadel, a state-supported, all-male military college in his home state, would have to admit women.

Yes, if The Citadel was a public school, the proposed law would require it to admit women, Mr. Bayh told him.

To Mr. Thurmond, that was the wrong answer. He couldn't imagine The Citadel with females. He abruptly turned on Mr. Bayh's proposal. Using the rules in place at the time, Mr. Thurmond insisted that the sex discrimination proposal wasn't relevant to the bill under discussion.

instant replay

Don't Call Me Bob

Growing up in the 1960s, Dorothy Richardson was the queen of the tetherball court and the fastest kid on the playground rings. When her older brother's friends wanted to play soccer, they asked her to be the goalie.

There were no girls' teams for her to play on, but her dad let her be the bat-girl for her brothers' Little League teams.

She dreamed about playing on a real team in a real league. "I would actually pray at night, 'God, why did you give me this talent when there's no opportunity?'" she remembered. "As much as I had this desire to play, society threw back at me, 'Well, you're a girl. You're not supposed to want to play.'"

In 1972, when she was ten, she helped her brother, a catcher, warm up for his Little League games by pitching to him. A coach raced over to her. "Wow, you've got a great arm," he told her. "How would you like to play on my Little League baseball team?"

Dorothy was elated. This was her big chance!

But the coach quickly burst her bubble. Girls weren't allowed in Little League. So he told her, "We're going to have to cut your hair short and we're going to give you a boy's name. We're going to call you Bob."

Bob? Dorothy didn't want to be a boy—or pretend to be one. She just wanted a chance to play baseball. She turned the coach down.

Soon after, she happened onto a women's fast-pitch softball team and was invited to join in. By the time she was a teenager, Dorothy "Dot" Richardson had become one of the best female softball players in the nation. She would go on to win two Olympic gold medals and become an orthopedic surgeon.

But she knows that her experience was rare. Her friends who played on boys' teams as teens usually had nowhere to go after that. Their sports careers were cut short.

"Isn't it a shame," she asked, "that we had to have a law for people just to express the gifts they've been given?"

Left: Dorothy "Dot" Richardson as a member of the Union Park Jets, around 1971.

45

Edith Green still had a problem to resolve.

The Senate parliamentarian, the official rule keeper, looked over the bill and agreed. The Senate wouldn't discuss it any further that day.

Mr. Bayh was distressed. He thought the parliamentarian's ruling was "ridiculous." But he had been caught by surprise, and no amount of oration would change the result. The Senate moved on to other matters.

Through the fall of 1971, Mr. Bayh would try again and again to bring the proposal up, without any luck.

Finally, at the end of February 1972, a persistent Mr. Bayh had another chance. The education bill came up once again, and Mr. Bayh again offered his proposal to ban sex discrimination in schools. This time, he was ready to appease his opponents. Military schools would be exempt from the law, at least for now—not because Mr. Bayh thought they should be, but because, shrewdly, he wanted the votes of Mr. Thurmond and others.

This time, his proposal passed. The section known as Title IX was finally in both the House and Senate education bills.

From there, Title IX should have cruised into law. But Edith Green still had a problem to resolve.

The Senate version of the education bill was very different from the House version. In particular the Senate took a different approach to financial aid for college students, one that Mrs. Green thought was unworkable and too expensive. To iron out the differences between the two bills, a conference committee was formed with members from both chambers. Mrs. Green was on the committee, but she didn't have many supporters within the group.

Off and on over several weeks, the committee worked out compromises on many issues. Title IX was actually toughened a bit. The committee agreed with the Senate that Title IX would apply to all admissions at state

Below: U.S. Representative Martha W. Griffiths *(left)* and Bella Abzug *(right)* on the day the House approved the 1971 Equal Rights Amendment.

instant replay

The Fight for Equal Rights

As 1970 approached, women's rights activists, disappointed with court rulings and slow progress, concluded the time had come for a more dramatic law—an amendment to the U.S. Constitution.

The Equal Rights Amendment would guarantee women would have the same rights as men had. Though the ERA had been introduced in every session of Congress since 1923, it had died in a congressional committee every time.

As she had with the Civil Rights Act of 1964, Martha Griffiths stepped up. There was only one way to get a bill out of a committee when the committee refused to act: A majority of the members of the House of Representatives—at least 218 of them—would have to sign a special discharge petition. This was a rare and risky maneuver that was tried only occasionally, and usually failed. If the tactic didn't work, the amendment might molder in the committee without any attention for many more years.

Figuring a petition was her only chance to have the ERA considered by the House, Mrs. Griffiths began calling and cajoling her colleagues in June 1970. One by one, she convinced more than seventy-five House members to sign the petition.

Women's organizations were given lists of representatives, so supporters could barrage them with phone calls and letters urging them to sign the petition. Gradually the list of signatures grew and grew.

On July 20, House Majority Leader Hale Boggs added his name to the petition. There were now two hundred signatures. Only eighteen to go!

Mrs. Griffiths left the floor for a moment. When she returned, she was shocked to see a line had formed in front of the petition. Now that so many people had signed, a group of politicians rushed to make sure *their* names were on the list before it was too late. Seventeen Republicans and one more Democrat signed to bring the total to 218.

Fifty years after women won the right to vote, the Equal Rights Amendment would finally be considered—and approved—by the House. But it wouldn't pass the Senate that year. The next year the House again overwhelmingly approved the ERA, just a few weeks before it considered Title IX. The Senate approved the law in 1972.

The ERA was broad in scope, covering everything Title IX addressed and much more. But before the Constitution could be amended, thirty-eight of the nation's fifty state legislatures would have to ratify the ERA. From the point of view of someone in 1972, this was the law that mattered, the one that would surely change the lives of American women.

The next few years would tell a different story.

Above: Girls often joined their mothers and other women at rallies and demonstrations calling for equal rights. Here, a girl participates in a 1971 march.

universities but sided with the House in excluding undergraduate admissions at private universities. Harvard could still discriminate but the University of Massachusetts could not.

On the last day, when key financial aid issues would be discussed, Mrs. Green got up at 4:00 A.M. to prepare, as she often did when a major confrontation was ahead. She arrived at the afternoon meeting ready to make her case. The committee wrestled with the issues late into the night.

At midnight Mrs. Green asked that the group adjourn for some rest. The chairman refused. All night Mrs. Green defended her position, but she felt as though even the House members on the committee were stacked against her. As the sun rose on the next day an exhausted Mrs. Green realized that she would lose her fight to keep the House version of the financial-aid piece intact.

At 5:00 A.M. she walked out. "I just said there was no use in doing this," she said later. "I really was very sick about it."

In Mrs. Green's absence, the committee approved a bill that Mrs. Green opposed. "I think this was the most disillusioning experience I've had in twenty years," she said.

instant replay

The Senate approved the final version in May 1972.

Upset and angry, Mrs. Green felt betrayed. Of course, she was pleased to have Title IX in the final bill. But she believed the joint House–Senate committee had completely ignored other crucial parts of the bill that the House had originally approved. To her, the financial-aid package in the final bill was all wrong. The busing provisions didn't represent the House's position.

She had tirelessly worked for two years to write legislation, to get it passed, and to win support for a section that would give females an equal opportunity in school. But the end result wasn't acceptable to her.

Always a woman of her convictions, Mrs. Green saw only one ugly but necessary option: She would ask the House to defeat the bill and start over. Title IX would have to wait for another day.

When the final vote came up on June 8, 1972, Mrs. Green was given only seven minutes to address the House. In that short amount of time, she couldn't explain the political

maneuvering that had led to such an
unfair result. She couldn't detail the
many failings she saw in the final bill.
So she decided to be straightforward
and blunt.

"I now find myself in the most
regrettable position of opposing the
legislation I originally cosponsored,"
she said. The bill is too costly and it
makes promises it cannot keep, she
went on, concluding, "Mr. Speaker, I
cannot vote for the conference
report."

When the time came, Mrs. Green
voted against her own bill.

Despite her strong words, the
House approved it, 218–180.

On June 23, 1972, President Nixon
signed the Education Amendments
of 1972 into law, making official the
first legislation to ensure equal access
to education for both sexes.

News accounts focused on the
busing issues and financial aid. The
New York Times devoted one sentence
to the part of the law calling for an
end to discrimination against women
in admissions. The *Washington Post*'s
only mention was in a second story
inside the paper. The piece known as
Title IX was practically invisible.

It wouldn't stay that way for long.
Quietly, a new era had begun for girls
and women. In many ways, the easy
part was over.

chapter 6

changing
THE rules

In the early 1970s, tennis star Billie Jean King felt
feminist activist and *Ms.* magazine editor Gloria Steinem
didn't recognize the significance of sports to women or
its power to highlight equal-rights issues.

"You should use us more," Ms. King urged Ms. Steinem.
Ms. Steinem replied, "Billie, this is about politics."
"Gloria," Ms. King replied, "we *are* politics."
—Retold in the *Washington Post*

Title IX carried all kinds of promise for
girls and women. But schools and universities needed to know precisely
what this law required of them.

Below: Caspar W.
Weinberger,
secretary of Health,
Education, and
Welfare, meets
with President
Richard M. Nixon
in the Oval Office
in 1974.

The job of interpreting the specifics of the law—and figuring out exactly what Congress wanted—went to the U.S. Department of Health, Education, and Welfare, known as HEW. Normally, the department would draft rules, ask the public for comment, and then publish the requirements, a process that generally took six months or perhaps a year.

But HEW was in no hurry this time. It had never dealt with sex discrimination issues before or even looked at classrooms and school activities in terms of how girls and boys were treated. The process was slow, said Caspar W. Weinberger, secretary of HEW at the time, because "we recognized what a change this was going to be."

After hearing from school and college officials and various women's groups, HEW's staff began to draw up regulations in late 1972. The process crawled along. The new law wasn't high profile or a high priority, and many schools weren't very enthusiastic about

it. There were other distractions. This was an election year. The long war in Vietnam finally appeared to be nearing an end. And many people in Washington were concerned about the implications of a burglary of a political office that became known as the "Watergate" scandal.

Sometime in mid-1973, HEW staffers asked Mr. Weinberger whether the new law would apply to gym classes and competitive sports. It seemed obvious to some that if the law prohibited special treatment for one sex, it would have to apply to a school activity that was mostly male. Yet sports weren't just any activity; they were a significant part of American culture and came attached to deeprooted and heartfelt feelings about what made boys boys and girls girls.

Girls and women had been playing organized sports in the United States for nearly a century, but their participation had nearly always been controversial. Not long after basketball was invented in 1891, some women

scorecard 1972–73

	1971-72	1972-73
Boys in high-school varsity sports	3,666,917	3,770,621
Girls in high-school varsity sports	294,015	817,073
Men entering medical schools	10,435	11,319
Women entering medical schools	1,653	2,251
Men in law schools	85,554	89,534
Women in law schools	8,914	12,173
Men in veterinary schools	5,158	5,355
Women in veterinary schools	702	888

Opposite: Cross-country champion Doris Brown Heritage, running in the 1970s.

player profile

Doris Brown Heritage, Cross-Country Champion

From the time she was very young, Doris Brown loved to run. Growing up in the country in the 1940s and 1950s, she would hop out of bed in the morning and run down to the beach or jog into the woods.

At her high school in Gig Harbor, Washington, the only sports teams were for boys. Girls weren't even allowed on the track that the boys practiced on. It never occurred to Doris that she should protest. "The highlight of my high school running career," she said, "was getting to go on the bus one time and watch the boys in their meet."

Doris yearned to run for a running club in Tacoma, but her parents were uncomfortable with such a tomboy. If she had that much energy, they told her, she should use it to work in the family's enormous garden.

Finally, after a year of begging, her parents gave in. She honed her skills running up and down the road after school in her saddle shoes and practicing in a long-jump pit dug into the family's garden. By the time she finished high school in 1960, she was one of the fastest female distance runners in the nation.

As she put herself through college and then went to work, she continued to compete in regional and national meets, paying for all her shoes, uniforms, and travel expenses. Men who saw her work out around the town's lake jeered at her and tried to shove her in the water.

Still, she persisted. Over the years she won six national and five world cross-country championships in relative obscurity. "Most of us feel that being second-class citizens would be a great advance," she once told a reporter. "Second-class citizenship sounds good when you are accustomed to being regarded as fifth-class."

physical education teachers devised a six-player girls' version, made up of three offensive and three defensive players. The girls' game was slow and cumbersome. Players couldn't cross the half-court line, offensive players could dribble only three times before they had to pass, and all players were forbidden from such masculine behavior as snatching the ball from opponents.

Senda Berenson, the creator of the girls' game, thought females were better suited for a gentler game than the rowdy male version. She worried that "the great desire to win and the excitement of the game will make our women do sadly, unwomanly things." For young men, "a certain amount of roughness is deemed necessary to bring out manliness," she wrote in a 1901 basketball guide. "Surely, rough play can have no possible excuse in our young women."

In the 1920s, after winning the right to vote, young women jumped eagerly into sports like golf, tennis, baseball, and track. The older generation was appalled—the women more than the men. One argument in the push for

instant replay

Women in the Olympics

When the Olympic Games were revived in 1896, women weren't included. According to one popular story, an ambitious Greek woman, Melpomene, petitioned to run the marathon but was turned away. Instead, she ran the race unofficially, starting out of view and paralleling the course, finishing well behind the top runner.

Women joined the games slowly, but in time they found them to be the perfect place to gain international fame as athletes. The first women Olympic athletes participated in the ladylike sports of tennis, golf, and yachting in 1900 and in swimming and diving in 1912. They began to compete in gymnastics and track in 1928—over the protests of some American physical educators, who feared that running, in particular, would ruin their femininity and fertility.

The debate grew after several women running the 800-meter race in 1928 dramatically collapsed onto the track after competing. The *New York Times* reported that, completely exhausted, they "fell headlong to the ground." For decades after, women were forbidden from running races longer than 1,500 meters for fear their bodies were too fragile.

Gradually, more women's sports would be added to the Olympic competition, including basketball in 1976 and soccer and softball in 1996. But perhaps the greatest breakthrough was in Los Angeles in 1984, when the women's marathon was finally added. Joan Benoit, a homegrown girl from Maine, won the race easily, ending the debate about female endurance once and for all.

instant replay

Little League

In 1972, Maria Pepe was selected for a Hoboken, New Jersey, Little League team. When parents on opposing teams objected, Little League officials ordered that she be dropped—or the Hoboken team would lose its chance to play.

"I was stripped of my uniform because I was a girl, not because of an inability to play," she said. "I couldn't stand up for myself, and that really hurt."

Over the years many such orders had come from Little League's Williamsport, Pennsylvania, headquarters, and the girls had simply been dismissed. But Maria's local NOW chapter filed a protest with the state, arguing that Little League used public fields and accepted public funds. As a result, the chapter argued, it should be open to all kids.

Little League officials, infuriated by the intrusion into their business, testified that girls were weaker than boys and their bones more fragile, making the game too dangerous for them. But other experts countered that the differences between boys and girls were few between the ages of eight and twelve years old.

A state hearing officer agreed with the girls. "The institution of Little League is as American as the hotdog and apple pie," she ruled. "There is no reason why that part of Americana should be withheld from girls."

In protest, most of the state's two thousand teams suspended operations while Little League appealed to the New Jersey Superior Court. The league didn't get the win it wanted. In March 1974 the judges voted 2 to 1 to allow girls to play.

That year, Little League directors changed their rules. They finally allowed girls to play, saying they would "defer to the changing social climate."

Right: Girls in Hoboken, New Jersey, 1974, are eager and ready to sign up for Little League.

"Is there anything you don't play?" "Yeah," she replied. "Dolls."

women to vote was that women were quite different from men, not necessarily equal to them, and that society was missing out on their special and unique qualities by shutting them out of public life. In that same vein, female physical education teachers firmly believed that the male style of play was not only unladylike, but also too strenuous for the "weaker sex," potentially preventing them from bearing children. Friendly games, where everyone could join in, were fine. But intense, high-level competition, they believed, would ruin a woman's moral and physical health.

In the mid-1920s a group of women physical educators effectively quashed competitive high school and college sports for girls. For many decades, girls' only real chance to compete would come on occasional "Play Days" with neighboring schools.

Outside of schools, amateur leagues sprang up, usually sponsored by companies looking for inexpensive publicity. Skills mattered in these leagues, but not as much as the players' looks, their uniforms, and the shape of their bodies. In 1926 a controversy over the short shorts worn by basketball players on an Employers Casualty insurance company team in Dallas helped boost game attendance, normally under two hundred, to five thousand spectators!

Out of that era came one of the best American athletes of all time. Mildred "Babe" Didrikson was recruited to play basketball for Employers Casualty before she finished high school in Beaumont, Texas. Dabbling in track on the side, she was a one-woman championship team at the national Amateur Athletic Union competition in 1932, entering eight events and winning five outright. (She actually tied for first place in the sixth event.) That earned her a trip to the 1932 Olympics in Los Angeles, where she won gold medals in the javelin throw and the 80-meter hurdles and silver in the high jump.

After the Olympics she played baseball and basketball before settling on golf. Her versatility was amazing. "Is there anything you don't play?" she once was asked.

"Yeah," she replied. "Dolls."

Despite her enormous success, male sportswriters criticized her short hair and her boyish trousers. One sportswriter called her a "Muscle Moll," an insulting term for a gangster's girlfriend. He argued that women should join in sports that offered cute costumes and made them look pretty,

rather than activities that made them sweat. "A girl just can't do those things and still be a lady," he wrote.

Later, Babe Didrikson would try to soften her image, marrying wrestler George Zaharias and wearing dresses and makeup as she won one ladies' professional golf tournament after another. But her competitiveness never faltered. In 1938 and 1945, she played in men's professional golf tournaments, and she continued to compete and win even after surgery for the cancer that ultimately killed her in 1956 at age forty-five.

For girls in public schools in the 1950s and 1960s, though, the gym was mostly off-limits. Tara VanDerveer, who would become one of the nation's

best women's basketball coaches, came to resent the boys' Little League teams and their junior high, junior varsity, and varsity basketball teams. In the mid-1960s she craved the chance to play basketball. But her junior high career lasted all of one day: In seventh grade she was allowed to join the high school girls on a "Play Day" with other schools.

The closest she got to a school team in junior high was watching the boys play. To convince her parents to take her to games, she volunteered to be the team mascot. Wearing a heavy bear suit, she often became so engrossed watching the game from the sidelines that she forgot to rally the crowd. That intensity helped her

Opposite: Mildred "Babe" Didrikson shows her form, clearing a hurdle in 1932.

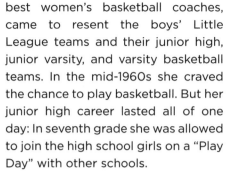
WOMEN ARE GETTING A RAW DEAL

Left: A series of groundbreaking articles in *Sports Illustrated* in 1973 highlighted the second-class treatment of female athletes.

59

later but it didn't make her much of a school mascot.

In the 1960s, as women began to speak out for more opportunities, attitudes started to change. The American Medical Association, which had warned for years that strenuous competition might be harmful to girls, finally reversed itself and recommended more vigorous activity. Over that decade some high schools and colleges started girls' teams—but almost halfheartedly.

Schedules were limited and girls' coaches were frequently volunteers, while boys' coaches were paid. Practices were scheduled late at night or early in the morning, when the boys didn't need the gym. Girls often got the boys' hand-me-down equipment and uniforms or had to raise money to buy their own. While the boys traveled to games by bus or even plane, girls usually had to form car pools and chip in for the gas.

When Christine H. B. Grant arrived in the United States in the late 1960s from Scotland via Canada, she remembers that "young girls were actively discouraged from participating in sports." The longtime athlete, who would become women's athletic director at the University of Iowa, said

family members would ask why women would want to do something that men do. Classmates made crude comments, calling female athletes "tomboys" or accusing them of being "lesbians," an especially derogatory label at the time. "Believe me, that was discouragement," said Ms. Grant. Girls and women, she said, "were fighting against every stereotype."

Then, in a most surprising way, one person—and one event—would help transform the way men and women looked at athletic girls.

Billie Jean King was one of the best women tennis players of the day and an outspoken advocate for women's rights. In 1970, when women tennis pros were receiving far less prize money than men, she and eight others broke away from the tennis establishment to form a women's tour, demanding bigger paydays. In 1971 she became the first female athlete to earn $100,000 in a single season.

Ms. King's forceful battles to win respect for women's tennis caught the attention of Bobby Riggs, a longtime tennis pro and publicity seeker who had won Wimbledon and the U.S. Open years before. A self-described "male chauvinist pig," Mr.

One event would help transform the way men and women looked at athletic girls.

Riggs was a blunt critic of feminism in general and women in sports in particular. "If a woman wants to get in the headlines, she should have quintuplets," he would say. The women's tennis game was boring and second-rate, he insisted. Men were far superior in strength, skill, and competitive intensity. And like many men, he believed any man could beat any woman, even a young professional at the top of her game. To prove his point, the fifty-five-year-old Mr. Riggs challenged the twenty-nine-year-old Ms. King to a match.

She refused. She didn't have time. And, truth be told, she didn't want to lose.

Undaunted, Mr. Riggs convinced another top women's player, the Australian Margaret Court, to play him in a match on Mother's Day, 1973. He trounced her.

When she heard the news, Billie Jean King knew she had to play Bobby Riggs and prove him wrong.

That summer the two agreed to play each other in a "Battle of the Sexes" on September 20, 1973. They would play a manly best-of-five match, instead of the usual best-of-three the women played, and the winner would take home $100,000. In one way, the match was a giant publicity stunt. But to many people, much more was on the line: If Billie

Above: Bobby Riggs shows off his muscles to Billie Jean King as part of the promotion leading up to their historic match.

Jean won, women might finally earn
credibility as athletes. If Bobby won,
women would never hear the end of
it. Men forever would point out their
athletic superiority, and women athletes might never earn respect for
their abilities.

In Las Vegas the oddsmakers
favored Mr. Riggs.

With the battle for the ERA and
other women's issues raging across
the country, Ms. King believed that far
more than a game was at stake. "It
was very clear this was about social
change and not about tennis," she
said. She tried to visualize what the
world would be like if she lost, and it

frightened her into practicing harder.

"I did everything I could to win
that match," she said, including hitting hundreds of overhead shots each
day and focusing on her volley, on
making her opponent move around.
She lifted weights to strengthen her
legs. She stayed up late and slept in
so that she would be prepared for the
evening event.

When the night came, the atmosphere in the Houston Astrodome was
like a circus sideshow on steroids.
Before a crowd of more than thirty
thousand, Mr. Riggs came on the court
in a rickshaw pulled by his female
"Bosom Buddies." Men in togas car-

ried out Ms. King in a sedan chair. Mr. Riggs gave her a giant Sugar Daddy candy bar. She gave him a baby pig. More than forty million people worldwide watched on television.

Despite the initial partylike atmosphere, the actual match had the intensity of a world-championship game. Both played hard, trying to outsmart the other. But by the end of the first set Ms. King had taken over. She was quick and strong, and his legs were not. As she placed her shots from one side of the court to the other, Mr. Riggs couldn't keep up. Billie Jean didn't just beat Bobby. She thrashed him, winning three straight sets, 6–4, 6–3, 6–3.

Over the next several weeks girls around the country rushed to buy tennis rackets and take up sports. Overnight, they saw themselves in a different light—powerful, emboldened, capable. Billie Jean King had shown the world: Girls could play hard too.

In the midst of the excitement, Washington regulators were wrestling with whether this new Title IX required boys and girls to share

player profile

Billie Jean King, Tennis Superstar

As a youngster, Billie Jean Moffitt played football with the other kids in the neighborhood and softball in a park league. But when she was ten years old, her mother retired her young halfback, declaring that football was "unladylike."

Figuring her softball career would soon end as well, she asked her dad what sports she could do. Golf, swimming, or tennis, he suggested. She chose tennis and soon was playing every day. By high school she was playing at Wimbledon.

The disparities between men and women hit home during her years at Cal State, Los Angeles. She was able to practice with the men. But she had to juggle two jobs to pay her way through, passing out equipment and working as a playground director.

Her boyfriend and future husband, Larry King, had half an athletic scholarship, though he joked he was the seventh man on a six-man tennis team.

One day they were walking hand in hand by the tennis courts, she recalled, and "he said, 'Do you realize you're a second-class citizen?' And I said, 'What do you mean?'"

At that point Billie Jean was one of the top tennis players in the world. "You're the best athlete, and you're the best-known person in the school," he told her. "Yet you're the one who has to work two jobs, and I get a grant. And the reason is you're a girl, you're a woman."

"That's the moment," she said, that "I became a true feminist."

Panel 1: HOWIE, DO YOU KNOW WHO BILLIE JEAN KING IS? SURE, SILLY!

10-24

Panel 2: WELL, WHEN I GROW UP, I'M GOING TO BE A TENNIS PLAYER, JUST LIKE HER!

Panel 3: ME, TOO! ME, TOO! I WANNA GROW UP TO BE A PROFESSIONAL TENNIS PLAYER, JUST LIKE *BILLIE JEAN KING!*

Panel 4: HOWIE! BREAK-THROUGH! WHAT? WHAT'D I SAY?

locker rooms and gym classes and whether schools now had to offer sports for girls as well as boys. Deciding on separate locker rooms was easy enough, but the crucial call on sports teams ultimately fell to Secretary Weinberger, who had taken a particular interest in this new law. He was a political conservative who had long opposed big government and heavy-handed meddling in people's business.

At the same time, he wasn't wowed with the athletic culture. Growing up, he had been a sickly kid who focused more on his studies than sports. Quipped one HEW staffer, "I don't think Weinberger ever played anything other than library."

Mr. Weinberger also sincerely believed everyone deserved an equal shot at all aspects of education. As he listened to arguments on both sides of the sports issue in 1973, he found the disparities glaring and unacceptable. Schools provided facilities, coaches, uniforms, and locker rooms for boys and men. But if girls and women wanted a team, he said, the attitude was, *Why, go raise money yourself.*

To him, it wasn't right that girls had to hold bake sales in order to play while boys didn't. It wasn't right that an estimated fifty thousand men went to college on athletic scholarships compared with perhaps fifty women. Though it was a controversial call, he concluded that sports teams were school activities covered under Title IX. If boys got to play, then girls should get to play too.

That single decision would change the course of the new law—and of American sports.

Above: A 1973 "Doonesbury" cartoon, noting the impact of the King–Riggs contest.

crying foul

"Impending doom is around the corner if these regulations are implemented."
—Walter Byers, NCAA Executive Director, talking about Title IX rules, 1974

Below and upper right: Buttons worn by Title IX supporters.

Officially, Title IX went into effect in June 1973, a year after it became a law. But HEW continued to dawdle on publishing the specific rules that would go with it.

In November 1973, almost accidentally, the word dribbled out that the new law might involve sports. Members of the National Collegiate Athletic Association, or NCAA, the powerful organization that coordinated men's college sports, attended a meeting of the fledgling coordinator for women's sports, the Association for Intercollegiate Athletics for Women, or AIAW, and heard a presentation on the possible Title IX athletics rules.

To NCAA members, this news was a nasty surprise. None of them had considered this possibility. While many schools had added a few women's teams, college athletic directors could hardly imagine a

women's sports program that might be on par with the men's. They didn't have the money for it. Besides, hardly any women seemed to play sports—or be interested in them.

As the NCAA quickly relayed the frightening discovery to college athletic directors and coaches around the country, a storm of opposition developed. NCAA representatives, universities, and their athletic directors bombarded HEW with letters and visits to try to convince staffers that the Title IX rules would destroy college sports.

In fact, the rules did threaten the athletics programs of the early 1970s. College sports were a huge business built almost exclusively around men. At the University of Michigan, $2.6 million a year was spent on men's sports. The budget for women's sports was $0—there was no women's varsity program. At the University of Washington, where more than four of ten undergraduates were female, the annual athletic budget was about $2 million. Just $18,000 of that amount went to women's varsity sports.

High school athletics, while less of a business, were equally focused on boys. In Fairfax County, Virginia, the school system spent $9 on boys' teams for every $1 on girls' sports. Parents and coaches had to mow and line the girls' softball fields. Girls' teams were left out of pep rallies and the morning announcements of the previous night's scores.

In Waco, Texas, the local school district spent $250,000 a year to field seven competitive boys' sports but just $970 to support the sole girls' sport, tennis. The *Washington Post* reported that athletic competition there, especially in football, was seen "not only as a builder of men, but also as a source of civic pride."

What about sports for girls? "It's not part of our culture in Waco," a school board member said.

The regulators at HEW weren't especially sympathetic to the NCAA.

Though college coaches and athletic directors were celebrities at their own schools, they were just another special-interest group to the more cerebral HEW staffers. Many of the HEW officials also were fathers of daughters, and they knew firsthand how girls were shut out.

Worried that HEW would actually adopt the rules, the NCAA and its members also turned to Congress and found support from John Tower, a senator from football-crazy Texas. In May 1974, on a relatively slow day in the Senate, Mr. Tower quietly proposed changing a pending education bill to insist that Title IX rules couldn't apply to any sports that brought in money from ticket sales. His explanation was brief: The sports that brought in money—mainly football and basketball—needed that money to pay for their coaches, scholarships, and travel. Forcing football programs

scorecard 1975–76

	1971–72	1975–76
Boys in high-school varsity sports	3,666,917	4,109,021
Girls in high-school varsity sports	294,015	1,645,039
Boys playing football	932,691	1,132,171
Girls playing volleyball	17,952	240,605
Boys playing basketball	645,670	722,895
Girls playing basketball	132,299	404,902
Boys playing baseball	400,906	425,386
Girls playing softball	9,813	140,736
Boys playing soccer	78,510	115,811
Girls playing soccer	700	11,534
Boys in track and field	642,639	664,413
Girls in track and field	62,211	410,922

Above: A 1974 "Doonesbury" carton captures the attitude of the times about including women in men's games.

to share their revenue from ticket sales and television broadcasts would damage premier programs.

Mr. Tower's amendment generated little discussion, mainly because very few senators were present at the time. The amendment passed the Senate on a voice vote with just a handful of lawmakers voting.

This time, the women's groups were caught unprepared, and they were horrified at the idea. Taking football and basketball out of the equation would be like benching the best two players on a basketball team during a big game. Women wanted the chance to play sports. But how even could the balance be if the 105 spots on a football team at the time—and the 105 athletic scholarships that went with them—didn't count at all? How fair would the division be if millions of dollars were spent on football and basketball programs, leaving women's sports and the remaining men's sports to scramble for leftover funds?

Left: A Bill Sanders editorial cartoon in the *Milwaukee Journal* makes light of the response of many coaches to Title IX.

They could stop Mr. Tower's plan—but only if they acted quickly. The Tower amendment still had to survive a joint House and Senate conference committee before it could become a law. Women's activists hurriedly sought out Congress's Title IX supporters.

In conference committee discussions a few weeks later Senator Jacob Javits from New York came up with a solution to take the bite out of Mr. Tower's amendment. During a break in the discussions, he rushed from the meeting room to ask for help in quickly putting together the wording for his proposal. Margot Polivy, a lawyer who represented the AIAW,

was there, as was Shirley Chisholm, the New York representative.

Unable to find a place to write in the hallway, Ms. Polivy helped scratch out the wording of the compromise using Ms. Chisholm's back as a writing surface. The conference committee and Congress agreed that no sports would be excluded from the Title IX rules. But the law would require HEW rules to take into account the cost differences between sports, such as the differences between football uniforms and soccer equipment. Legislators also demanded that HEW finally publish rules for the two-year-old law.

In late June 1974, on a day when President Nixon was touring the Middle

instant replay

Looking for a Little Respect

Girls' sports teams were almost an afterthought at many schools in the 1970s. This June 1973 letter to *Ms. Magazine* summed up the frustration of many female athletes:

I am in the ninth grade and on the girls' varsity basketball team at our school. I'm captain of the team and lead it in scoring, steals, and assists. I love basketball.

During our whole season this year, we had only five games; we had to furnish rides to the games ourselves; we had to play in our gymsuits because we had no uniforms in which to play; we were able to use the gym only when the boys were through with it; and we had a grand total of about 30 spectators at all our games combined. Our principal did not

announce any of our games, and did not provide a late bus so that kids could stay and watch. One time I asked if it would be possible to get uniforms for our team. I was told to earn the money through car washes, dances, and bake sales. Yet each of the boys received brand-new $30 uniforms this year.

Everyone seems to think that girls playing basketball is a big joke, but I am dead serious. If we are good enough to be called varsity, aren't we good enough to be respected?

—*Jane L.*

Above: Caspar W. Weinberger outlining the new Title IX rules for the media in 1974.

East and lawmakers were looking into Watergate issues at home, Mr. Weinberger at last announced HEW's proposed rules for Title IX. Now, for the first time, most of the American public heard about the massive changes that would be required in the nation's schools. Males and females would have to be treated equally in admissions and teacher pay. Even fond old traditions would have to go: No longer could schools keep girls from becoming crossing guards or operating movie projectors.

Athletics, of course, was the hottest topic. At a press conference announcing the rules, Mr. Weinberger joked that "my mail tells me it is the most important subject in the United States today." The new rules called for males and females to have an equal opportunity to compete in sports, though schools did not have to spend the same amount on each sex. Females also would be entitled to the same quality of locker rooms, coach-

ing, travel, and equipment as males were. "I think the results will be that athletics as we know it will not be disrupted, but that there will be a substantially improved opportunity for women to participate in athletics," Mr. Weinberger told reporters.

Just announcing the rules didn't make them official. People needed a chance to comment on them. Then HEW had to make revisions and submit official regulations for the president's signature.

In the best of times, such bureaucratic rules typically generate a few hundred responses. This was no ordinary time: In August, President Nixon resigned amid growing outcry over the Watergate scandal, and Vice President Gerald Ford, a former U.S. representative from Michigan, was sworn in as president. Yet despite the national turmoil, the new Title IX rules drew nearly ten thousand comments from the public.

Some believed the rules went too far. Others wanted them to go much further by banning stereotypes in textbooks, which frequently painted boys as daring, smart, and aggressive and girls as passive, frail "sissies."

Even the women's rights activists struggled with what to do, especially

instant replay

Saving the Scouts

As regulators and lawmakers studied the impact of the new Title IX rules, some of them saw an unintended consequence. Groups that met on school property but admitted only boys or girls would be outlawed.

In public schools across America, Boy Scouts and Girls Scouts, Boys Clubs and Girls Clubs, and YMCAs and YWCAs might have to take their programs out of schools or drop them altogether. On college campuses, social fraternities and sororities, which provided housing and a social life at many universities, might become illegal.

To head off such a disaster, legislators adopted the first change to Title IX, which made clear that the Boys Scouts and Girls Scouts and college "Greeks" were not meant to be covered by the new law. In late 1974, during her last days in Congress, Edith Green supported the change in the House, while Birch Bayh marshaled it through the Senate.

Mr. Bayh, however, was careful to make a distinction in one of Title IX's very few changes. Congress was happy to let boys and girls and men and women split up for social reasons. But it did not allow single-sex honor societies or professional fraternities and sororities—those based on academic achievements—since students often looked to those groups to help them land jobs or get into graduate school. Those societies would have to accept both men and women.

on the sports issue. Cranking out reports on electric typewriters and meeting at one another's Washington offices, they spent hours debating how to weigh equal opportunity in sports. Should each school field just one team in each sport, with only the best boy and girl athletes? That probably would lead to teams that were mostly boys. Boys-only and girls-only teams weren't ideal either, since the teams would need to be "separate but equal." Though it was a hard standard to measure, the latter ultimately seemed like the best choice.

While regulators studied their options and polished the rules, more months ticked away. Edith Green, the mother of Title IX, retired after twenty years in Congress and returned to Oregon. The controversy over Title IX and athletics spilled onto the sports pages of local newspapers. With so much focus on athletics, other pieces of the civil rights law were almost ignored. In 1974 female admissions to law schools soared. Princeton University said it would no longer limit women to 300 of its 1,100 freshman spots and would accept them on an equal basis with men.

In May 1975, after much of another school year had passed, President Ford finally signed the Title IX rules, and Mr. Weinberger announced the final regulations. No longer could girls be restricted to home economics classes or boys to shop class. No longer could counselors give career-interest tests and hand different forms to boys and girls. Gone would be the pink forms for girls, which suggested that those interested in science try nursing, while the blue forms recommended that boys interested in science become doctors. Girls and boys would take PE together, giving girls access to the same playing fields the boys had long controlled. Schools could spend more on boys' sports than on girls' sports, but girls had to have a chance to play.

Under a special rule then in place, Congress had forty-five days—until late July—to sign off on the HEW regulations.

This time, both the NCAA and women's groups were ready for a showdown. The NCAA and its members contacted their legislators and allies. Meanwhile, a coalition of education and women's groups representatives, including the American Association of University Women (AAUW), the League of Women Voters, the National Federation of Business and Professional Women, the National Education Association, and NOW, agreed to work together to lobby Congress. Calling themselves the National Coalition for Women and Girls in Education, the group really consisted of a few dozen women, maybe one or two from each group. But their groups combined had more than 3.5 million female members nationwide. When they talked to lawmakers, the women pointed out that they represented millions of American girls and women. But in private they jokingly called themselves "the mythical marching millions."

Meanwhile, eight of the nation's most successful and popular football coaches, including Tom Osborne of the University of Nebraska, Bo Schembechler of the University of Michigan, and Darrell Royal, the long-time coach at the University of Texas, headed to Washington to warn Congress of the dangers of Title IX.

Below: The "Tank McNamara" cartoon strip by Jeff Millar and Bill Hinds was one of the first to support Title IX and women's sports. This one ran in 1975.

Coach Royal told the representatives that he believed women would benefit from sports just like men do. But, he said, if schools had to divide football and basketball funds to support women's sports as well, all of the programs would be damaged. "Any way we look at it, we can't see that it is going to do anything other than eliminate, kill, or seriously weaken the programs that we already have in existence," he said.

Later, Coach Royal, Coach Schembechler, and others would spend more than an hour meeting with President Ford, a former University of Michigan football player, to talk about the impact of the Title IX rules. They figured that as a former athlete and coach, the president, more than anyone in Washington, would hear and understand their position.

But both the president and Congress held firm on the HEW rules.

Then one last hurdle emerged. Bob Casey, a congressman from Texas, felt strongly that PE classes should be all-boys or all-girls. In late July 1975, just before the rules were to become effective, he tried to change Title IX to include a section specifically about PE classes. Patsy Mink managed the debate, which once again was heated

and emotional. To Title IX supporters, anything that weakened the rules for athletics would open the door for bigger changes later.

Midway through the debate Mrs. Mink suddenly left the House floor with tears in her eyes. Some newspapers reported that she was upset over the turn of events. That was far from true. Her daughter, Wendy, a graduate student at Cornell University, had been in a terrible car accident and was critically injured.

As a vote neared, the nineteen women in the House moved around the floor, encouraging their colleagues to oppose any change to Title IX. But without Mrs. Mink, Mr. Casey's amendment passed, 212–211. When the final tally came in, supporters of the change cheered and burst into applause. Maybe, they hoped, Title IX could be stopped after all.

The coalition of women's groups had seen enough. When they started working on Title IX, Bunny Sandler and her colleague Margaret Dunkle, Margot Polivy, and others had relatively little political experience. But over months of negotiating and lobbying for Title IX rules, they had honed their persuasive skills. Now they moved into full gear, swarming

Give women a
"Sporting Chance."

instant replay

Female Cadets

With attitudes toward women changing rapidly in the mid-1970s, Congress turned its attention to another taxpayer-supported male bastion: the U.S. military academies.

In late 1975, President Gerald Ford signed a law opening admissions in the U.S. Naval Academy, the U.S. Air Force Academy, and the U.S. Military Academy at West Point, New York, to "female individuals."

Among the many concerns were what uniforms the new students would wear. The Air Force Academy's tailor shop came up with a skirt, though slacks would be allowed in bad weather. At West Point a winter uniform would consist of a beret, wool skirt, overcoat, and cape. In the traditional dress uniform, designers cut out pockets and trimmed off the jacket's tails because, one officer explained, "they just stick out too much in back."

Changing the uniforms was easier than changing the military mind-set, however. The military academies trained students for combat. Many military officials worried that women couldn't handle the physical demands and feared standards might be lowered since women wouldn't be sent to the front lines of war. Military officials like Lieutenant General Sidney B. Berry, West Point's superintendent, initially threatened to resign if women were admitted. But as the arrival day for new students approached, he had his game face on. "It was rather adolescent on my part," he said of his threat. "But I got over it and decided to do what a good soldier does—get on with the job."

Left: A model shows off the new dress for the first West Point women in 1975.

73

Senate and House offices from early in the morning until late at night. They handed out literature in the hallways to lawmakers and key aides and mapped out tactics in the cafeterias. Wearing buttons reading GOD BLESS YOU, TITLE IX and GIVE WOMEN A "SPORTING CHANCE," they collared legislators and staff members on elevators to argue that Title IX needed to be left intact.

The all-male Senate sided with the women and declined to add a provision about PE classes to Title IX. Because the two had to agree, the House would have to reconsider its stance.

On July 18 the House took up the issue again, with several representatives reminding their colleagues of Mrs. Mink and her recent misfortune. The congresswoman herself remained at Wendy's bedside as her daughter began a long and painful recovery.

In pushing his change to the law, Mr. Casey noted, "I have never seen such lobbying in my life as there has been on this amendment." Despite the "vociferous and aggressive effort" by "very charming lobbyists," he said he wouldn't change his mind. "I love women," he said. "I have five daughters. I have a charming wife." But, he argued, HEW shouldn't tell schools how to run their PE classes.

Others offered a different personal view. Gladys Noon Spellman of Maryland recalled being asked to leave a high school forty-five years before because she had dared to run on a track with the boys. "Unless we have a little more enlightenment than some of the rhetoric indicates that we have," she warned, "my granddaughter will be asked to leave a high school because she too will have to run on the 'boys' track."

This time, the House voted down Mr. Casey's amendment, 215–178.

The *Washington Post* reported that House members bowed to pressure from "hundreds of women's rights lobbyists." More likely, it just *seemed* like hundreds of women. Said one: "There were only twenty-seven of us, but we were a talky bunch."

The victory was sweet. Soon after, a group of politicians and activists celebrated their lobbying success and the final rules with a big third birthday party for Title IX. There was a special reason to celebrate. The time had finally come for schools to change their ways.

The victory was sweet.

chapter 8
play ball!

"The stigma is nearly erased. Sweating girls are becoming socially acceptable."

—Liz Murphey, University of Georgia, women's athletics coordinator, 1978

Below: An article in the *Yale Daily News* on the rowing team's 1976 protest. Members of the women's rowing team, sans shirts, confronted school PE director, Joni Barnett, about their lack of basic facilities.

For months, the women on the crew team at Yale University had been asking for a place to shower after their practices. For the 1975–76 school year, a special trailer was ordered. But the school failed to get a special permit from the local community, so the trailer sat unused through the winter, without water or electricity.

Every day after practice the women sat on the bus, sweaty on the inside, cold and soaking wet on the outside, waiting for the male rowers to finish showering in the men's locker room at the boathouse. Then they would shiver through the bus ride back to the New Haven, Connecticut, campus, where they finally got showers. Several of the women became ill, one with pneumonia, but their request was still ignored.

Finally, the team members ran out of patience. Clearly, they needed to do something dramatic or they would never get their showers. On March 3, their faces grim and their moods tense, twenty women marched silently to the office of Joni Barnett, the school's PE director. There, crowded

Oarswomen bare all, want March showers

Yesterday afternoon twenty women marched into the office of Joni Barnett, director of physical education, and their leader said, "Mrs. Barnett, we have something to show you."

Indeed they did. The varsity women's crew doffed their sweatsuits and stood naked before Barnett as Captain Chris Ernst, 1976, read a statement protesting the lack of shower and changing facilities for women at the Derby Boathouse.

"On a day like today the ice freezes on this skin," the statement said. "Then we sit for half an hour on the bus as the ice melts and soaks through our suits to meet the sweat that's soaking us from the inside.

"We sit for half an hour with the chills....half a dozen of us are sick now."

Last year, the University rented a trailer with four working shower heads. This year there is a new trailer with twice the capacity, but it has not been hooked up to an electric line because the athletic department did not obtain the necessary zoning variance.

Until Tuesday's special meeting of the Derby Zoning Committee, the women must do without showers.

"Joni Barnett was asked in November to obtain a variance," asserted crew member Anne Warner, 1977, "and reminded in December, January, and February. And still there is no variance."

The crew chose Barnett as the object of their dissatisfaction, because, according to the statement, "(Barnett) is the symbol of women's athletics at Yale." They acted without the prior knowledge of their coach, Nat Case.

Athletic Department Reacts

Joni Barnett expressed surprise over

—continued on page ten

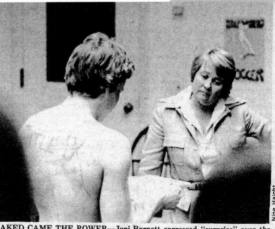

NAKED CAME THE ROWER—Joni Barnett expressed "surprise" over the women's crew demonstration yesterday, but her countenance reveals something sadder.

Nina Haight

into her small office, the women stripped off their shirts. TITLE IX was written in Yale blue on their bare chests and backs.

Team captain Chris Ernst read a statement that began, "These are the bodies Yale is exploiting." A photographer from the *Yale Daily News*, who had been alerted to the protest, caught the moment on film for the school newspaper. The *New York Times* reported it the next day, and the demonstration got national attention.

The protest rattled Yale athletic officials. The athletic director called the situation "a crisis" and made arrangements to get the permit approved within days so the trailer could be used. Appalled alumni offered cash donations for a new women's locker room, and the university promised the women boathouse facilities similar to the men's. Still, the athletic director called the display "the most God-awful thing I've ever heard of."

Voluntarily and involuntarily, schools across the country began responding to Title IX in the second half of the 1970s, gradually adding sports for girls and women and slowly opening vocational programs. HEW had given high schools one year and colleges up to three years to comply with its Title IX rules, and it asked the nation's 2,700 colleges and 16,000 public schools to sign a form agreeing to comply with the rules.

Female admissions to colleges and graduate programs picked up speed, driven by female ambition, the law, and a growing acceptance that it was simply wrong to reject someone just for being a girl. Between 1971 and 1976 the number of women attending college jumped 40 percent. By the fall of 1976 one in every four law students was a woman, up from about one in ten in 1971; likewise, a quarter of first-year medical students were female, up from about one in seven just five years before.

scorecard 1976–77

	1971-72	1976-77
Men playing in college sports	170,384	168,136
Women playing in college sports	29,977	62,886
Bachelor's degrees awarded to men	500,590	495,545
Bachelor's degrees awarded to women	386,683	424,004
Men entering medical schools	10,435	11,495
Women entering medical schools	1,653	3,771
Men in law schools	85,554	87,469
Women in law schools	8,914	29,982
Men in veterinary schools	5,158	5,198
Women in veterinary schools	702	2,045

Educators began to realize the long-lasting effects that old-fashioned attitudes had on girls. Some male teachers told girls they didn't need advanced high school math classes to be wives and mothers, and one teacher told a male struggling with a math concept, "You think like a girl." Some parents kept their daughters out of challenging math programs for fear the girls would appear too smart and would be teased. Driving the message home, one junior high math competition offered a tie clasp for first prize.

After hearing repeatedly that girls weren't very good at math, many girls failed to take four years of math in high school, leaving them without the right courses to study many subjects in college. Aware of this divide, teachers began to encourage girls to push through difficult math and science concepts and to stick with the subjects.

instant replay

The Warsaw Tigers

In 1976, Indiana, perhaps the nation's most basketball-crazy state, created its first statewide basketball tournament for girls. For the Warsaw High School girls' team, the tournament offered something to stretch for, a goal to dream about.

Led by guard Judi Warren, the seniors had lost only four games since their freshman year. But they didn't get much respect. They didn't have real uniforms or buses to their games, and they had to practice between 7 P.M. and 9 P.M., after the boys' varsity, reserve, and freshman teams practiced first.

One evening, team members approached Ike Tallman, the boys' coach, with a few demands—including equal access to the gym. His answer: When the girls filled the gym like the boys did, the two could share it. That was a daunting challenge. Only a few family members and close friends ever attended the girls' games.

When the season ended, though, the team was undefeated. The Tigers swept through the first round of the tournament, and then won the regional championship. Posters began to appear on the school walls, and fifteen hundred fans turned out for the next round.

When the Tigers won that, too, the school had a pep rally for them. Their classmates packed the gym. Toward the end, Mr. Tallman took the microphone. Looking toward the team, he told the crowd, "Some of you have been after me to share this gym, and I said no, not until you can fill it. Well, I owe you girls an apology . . . because I see you *can* fill this gym."

Led by Judi, the team went on to win the first Indiana girls' championship. Judi was named the state's first Miss Basketball, the year's top female player. And the next year, boys and girls took turns using the gym after school for practice.

THAT'S A NICE FOOTBALL YOU HAVE THERE, LINUS

SHALL I GIVE HIM THE STATISTICS, SIR?

9-25

IN 1978, THE AVERAGE BUDGET FOR INTERCOLLEGIATE ATHLETICS FOR MEN WAS $717,000, BUT FOR WOMEN IT WAS ONLY $141,000

© 1979 United Feature Syndicate, Inc.

✳SIGH✳

Above: A Charles Schulz "Peanuts" cartoon in 1979. Mr. Schulz was another early supporter of Title IX.

In athletics departments, budgets for girls' sports were doubling and tripling, though they were still a fraction of what was spent on boys' sports. In the 1975–76 school year more than 15,000 high schools had a girls' basketball team, triple the number of five years before. More than 10,000 schools had a girls' volleyball team, compared with 1,550 in 1971. Colleges began to offer women athletic scholarships.

Often, though, schools made the changes grudgingly. The male teams had a long tradition, built up over many years. Then, all of a sudden, girls and women were being handed varsity teams, though attendance at their games was awful and alumni financial support was nonexistent. After a Title IX complaint was filed at the University of Michigan, the school started six varsity sports for women, including tennis, basketball, and

synchronized swimming, and made plans for more. Women began to receive athletic scholarships. But male athletes and coaches could tolerate only so much. They balked at the newcomers earning the prestigious varsity letter "M." "Wouldn't you feel the letter would lose some of its meaning if you saw it on a member of the synchronized swimming team?" the varsity-level M Club wrote to its members. Months of angry debate followed before women finally got their "M."

At the University of Georgia the budget for women's sports grew to $120,000 in 1978 from $1,000 in 1973, but the men received $2.5 *million*. Among the differences: The men on the golf team got all the golf balls they needed. Women golfers got one for each competitive round they played. Michigan State University's women's basketball players practiced through dinnertime in a gym with little heat, often returning to their dorms after the dining halls had closed. And at schools as different as Freemont High School in inner-city Los Angeles and the giant University of Texas, uniforms had to be shared among different female teams.

"The volleyball team had to make sure they got back in time to wash their uniforms and give them to the basketball team," said Donna Lopiano, the women's athletic director at the University of Texas at the time. With her limited budget, she says, she gave the coaches "gas money and Tide."

Some schools still resisted adding girls' sports. A high school student in Mannington, West Virginia, wrote in 1976 that her school had five boys'

player profile

Donna de Varona, Champion *and* Activist

Olympic swimmer Donna de Varona first swam into Washington politics in the early 1970s, trying to call attention to the needs of Olympic athletes. Before long, she was campaigning for women athletes as well.

By then Ms. de Varona was nationally known, not just for her Olympic gold, but also for her role as a sports broadcaster for the ABC network. While attending the University of California, Los Angeles, she had begun working for ABC's *Wide World of Sports* TV series, becoming one of the very first female sports broadcasters. She was successful enough that she left school before graduating to focus on her work and didn't earn her degree until 1986.

In 1974 she helped Billie Jean King start the Women's Sports Foundation, perhaps the nation's most outspoken advocate for female athletes. Ms. de Varona became the foundation's first president.

In 1975 President Gerald Ford named her to a national commission to study the U.S. Olympic program, which was suffering from poor coordination and bickering among the many groups that sponsored various sports. After the committee issued its report in 1977, she left television to work full time in the U.S. Senate, helping Ted Stevens, a senator from Alaska, and others craft a law to aid amateur athletes.

The result was the Amateur Sports Act of 1978. Once, the U.S. Olympic Committee (USOC) had done little more than provide uniforms and make travel arrangements for American Olympians. But the new law refocused the USOC, giving it the power to coordinate all the different sports, pick Olympic teams, and run training centers for potential competitors—all measures aimed at helping American athletes reach their potential.

JUNE 26, 1978 $1.00

TIME

Moscow vs. Washington
The Spy War

Women In Sports

Above: As girls began to take the playing field in impressive numbers, the national news magazine *Time* took notice in 1978.

teams but none for girls. When she complained to the principal that girls wanted to play too, he suggested another way for her to satisfy her interest in sports: "Go watch the boys."

Teachers and women athletic directors who spoke out or demanded too much risked losing their jobs. In Colorado a woman athletic director at Colorado State University and a high school girls' PE teacher were both fired for trying to get more money and basic amenities for their female athletes. Juries later ordered the schools to pay damages to both

women for violating their freedom of speech.

Even with the challenges they faced, the women playing sports in college for the first time were frequently in awe that they had the chance at all. And girls in their teens began to expect opportunities that their big sisters never imagined.

Missy Parks remembers her older sister playing only six-player basketball in church leagues. But when Missy entered her parochial high school in Greenville, South Carolina, four years later, in 1976, a girls' basketball team was in place, as were volleyball, tennis, softball, and track teams. She played on most of them.

"I can't imagine my life without sports in high school," she says. "For me, it was a vaccine against all adolescent ills." She was too busy to watch TV or to get into trouble. On Friday nights, she often played pickup games at the local Y. Along the way she learned plenty of lessons about teamwork and dealing with failures and defeat.

She also found her career in her experience. After graduating from Yale, where she played five varsity sports, Missy founded a catalog company to sell women's athletic clothing. She named it Title 9 Sports, in part because of the difference Title IX made in her own life. She still plays basketball in a company league. "Sports for me established my place in the world," she says.

At the same time, the best female players were changing how the rest of the world looked at girls and their sports. In California, a phenomenon named Cheryl Miller lit up the basketball court. In grade school, she played pickup ball with the neighborhood boys, often teaming up with her younger brother, Reggie, who would become a standout player for the Indiana Pacers. In the late 1970s, however, Cheryl was the family star.

As a freshman at Riverside Polytechnic High School in 1978, she was named to the All-America team and realized for the first time that she might be able to attend college on an athletic scholarship. A prolific shooter

and rebounder, she once scored 105 points in a single game her senior year. Her family set aside a room for the recruitment letters and knickknacks received from the 250 schools that contacted her before she chose the University of Southern California. By contrast, the next year Reggie was pursued by just a handful of schools.

"I just came in on the whole wave of Title IX," she says.

As a new generation of female athletes began to rewrite the record books, Washington wrestled with how to apply the new law. The issue was still controversial, and the Department of Health, Education, and Welfare was pokey in investigating complaints, taking months or even years to respond. And when it did rule, it sometimes made the kinds of decisions that make government agencies the butt of comedians' jokes.

In 1976 an HEW regional office ruled that an all-boy choir discriminated

Below: Buttons from the 1970s.

instant replay

The ERA Fails

The Equal Rights Amendment got off to a quick start in 1972, the same year Title IX was passed. By early 1973 thirty state legislatures of the thirty-eight needed for passage had agreed that equal rights for women should be part of the United States Constitution. Winning over the remaining state legislatures before the 1979 deadline seemed relatively easy.

The amendment was short but powerful. "Equality of rights," it read, "shall not be denied" by the U.S. or any state "on account of sex."

But opposition, led by an articulate lawyer named Phyllis Schlafly, began to form and gather support. As legislatures in the remaining states considered the amendment, busloads of opponents rolled into state capitals, arguing that such a radical proposal would hurt women and upset the American way of life. The ERA, they said, would lead to a host of terrible results: Women would be drafted. Pregnant women would be sent to battlefields. Public bathrooms would be open to both sexes. Homemakers would be forced to work to provide part of the family income.

Most of these scenarios weren't likely, but fears that this amendment would overturn traditional male and female roles were real. Though a majority of Americans supported the ERA, only thirty-five states had ratified it as the deadline neared.

Congress agreed to extend the deadline until 1982. That wouldn't be enough. The amendment would fail, three states short of approval, and it wouldn't come up again.

The loss was a huge disappointment to many women who had worked for equal opportunity. But the issues they had raised were heard. Through new laws and court rulings, married women were able to get credit cards and bank loans and buy property without their husbands' signatures. Title IX outlawed quotas in education. Pregnant women were allowed to keep their jobs. Spurred by the prospect of an Equal Rights Amendment, many state and national laws were changed to give women more rights.

The issues they had raised were heard.

against girls, violating Title IX. Then, that July, HEW ruled that Scottsdale, Arizona, schools couldn't hold their traditional father-and-son banquets or mother-and-daughter teas.

President Gerald Ford was furious. He found the decision so outrageous that he ordered HEW to back off the very next day. "The President was really quite irritated," his press secretary told reporters.

In asking his fellow senators to support changes to Title IX, Birch Bayh, the original Senate sponsor of the law, accused HEW of going out of its way to make Title IX look silly. "Instead of really dealing with the fact that we are not getting equal scholarships, we are not getting equal course opportunities, we are not getting equal employment opportunities for our daughters, what do they do? They come up and say, 'You cannot have mother-daughter, father-son banquets.' That is the most idiotic thing I have ever heard."

The decisions were eventually reversed, but they left the impression that efforts to end sex discrimination had gone from reasonable to ridiculous. Congress quickly approved a second small change to Title IX, making clear that father-son and

Above: As the first deadline neared for states to approve the Equal Rights Amendment, people on both sides of the issue held rallies and demonstrations. Here, some Girl Scouts show support in 1977.

Right: A Jeff MacNelly editorial cartoon in 1976 made light of HEW's rulings on all-boy choirs and mother-daughter teas.

Below: HEW Secretary Joseph A. Califano Jr. with President Jimmy Carter in 1977.

mother-daughter events were perfectly okay, as long as programs were offered for both sexes. (It also included an exemption for beauty pageants, so that they could continue to offer scholarships for beauty queens.)

Following that skirmish, HEW turned almost silent. To avoid any other controversies, all Title IX decisions had to come from Washington.

The result? No decisions were made at all. For nearly a year between the summers of 1976 and 1977, HEW didn't even respond to its mail about Title IX, leaving some six hundred letters sitting unanswered in Washington.

After Jimmy Carter became president in 1977, women's groups pressured the new HEW secretary, Joseph A. Califano Jr., to fix Title IX enforcement. Mr. Califano looked for some quick and simple solutions.

Title IX had come to encompass all kinds of issues, including different dress codes for boys and girls. HEW had received a hundred complaints from students and parents arguing that girls shouldn't have to wear bras if boys didn't have to and that boys should be able to wear their hair long, just like girls could. He decided to leave dress codes to the schools so HEW could concentrate on more important issues.

instant replay

Edith Green, Critic

Edith Green entered Congress as a liberal, one who believes the government must be active in social policy, and left as a conservative, one who worries that too much government is bad for the country. She was proud of Title IX and its potential but uncomfortable and increasingly vocal about how regulators interpreted it.

In the mid-1970s she was openly critical of the rules for the law which "I drafted in the House, but whose parentage I am sometimes tempted to deny." She saw regulators require schools to fill out endless forms. She cringed at the "fertile imaginative brain" of bureaucrats who threatened to ban all-boy choirs and father-son banquets. The government was ordering that PE and other classes always include both sexes, when she believed schools should make that choice themselves.

"Regretfully," she said, "while Congress can write our common concerns into legislation, we cannot legislate the uncommon gift of common sense needed to administer laws intelligently."

She felt strongly that women should have the same access to sports and scholarships as men. But she opposed any kind of quotas, knowing that fixed requirements can cut both ways. "One of the ugliest aspects of discrimination was always the 'quota system'—quotas limiting women, blacks, Jews, persons of Irish descent," she often said. "Quotas represented the crudest form of mindless inequality, because that meant that an important decision was being made not on merit."

Despite her sharp words, she remained hopeful that her law would allow women to enter more professions, increase their paychecks, and reach their potential. "I've always felt that if you could give a woman or a young girl an equal opportunity in terms of education and equal pay and equal opportunities in work, that you really have done just about all that you are ever going to be able to do anyhow," she told an interviewer in 1978. "And then, if you can make every young girl know that there's no ceiling of expectations, that there is no height to which that young girl cannot go, she'll aspire to that."

In addition, thousands of the forms that colleges and public schools were supposed to fill out, agreeing to comply with the law, had been lost or accidentally destroyed. Many were in cardboard boxes or scattered on floors. No one knew who had signed a form and who hadn't. So one of Mr. Califano's first steps, which he called "mostly symbolic," was to send out new forms and actually file those that were returned.

The point was
human dignity.

There was another pressing matter: Though HEW had produced rules in 1975, it still needed to tell schools how they would know if they were complying with the law.

At first, Mr. Califano didn't understand why women activists were so cranked up about sports. Playing basketball in nice uniforms hardly seemed comparable to the disgraceful discrimination blacks faced during segregation. But in time he came to understand that "intercollegiate athletic programs were the lunch counters in the South for these women," he wrote later. "The point was human dignity." Why shouldn't women have the same chance as men to learn character and teamwork, to understand achievement and defeat?

In December 1978 he floated a proposal: Schools should spend roughly the same on each female athlete as they did on each male athlete.

University administrators and athletics officials had a quick answer: No way! Adding women's sports was costly enough. They couldn't begin to increase women's sports budgets to the same level as men's, especially if the costly football program was included.

About three hundred colleges, led by Duke University President Terry Sanford, banded together to fight the proposal. Margot Polivy, lawyer for the AIAW, remembered Mr. Sanford outlining the group's position. He explained that "he was all for equality." But, Ms. Polivy said, Mr. Sanford

Below: A "Tank McNamara" cartoon in 1979.

added, "we had to understand that there were three sexes in athletics: men, women, and football players."

As the outcry over his proposal grew Mr. Califano was summoned to a private meeting with leaders of the House of Representatives. In strong terms, they made clear that he was making a foolish mistake. They warned that the nation's legislators might dismantle Title IX or take away some of HEW's funding if he stuck to his proposal. Bill Ford, representative from Michigan, put it bluntly: "You can lose an election on the sports pages that you'll never lose on the front pages. And that's what you'll do with this interpretation."

Mr. Califano agreed to back off on his proposal. Not long after, President Carter fired him for opposing the president's plan to create a separate

Above: HEW Secretary Patricia Roberts Harris holds a photo of a different generation of women athletes as she discusses new standards for Title IX in 1979.

Department of Education. Patricia Roberts Harris, the new HEW secretary, had to finish the Title IX job.

By now Title IX had gotten the backing of many women athletes. One of the most outspoken was Donna de Varona, the Olympic gold medalist in swimming who had seen her own career cut short. Determined to help future athletes, she had lobbied since the mid-1970s for laws to support amateur athletes.

Ms. de Varona, race car driver Janet Guthrie, and other women athletes met with Ms. Harris and President Carter to urge them to finish the Title IX process. The new secretary held meeting after meeting with women's groups, the NCAA, and university officials and then came up with final guidelines that are still in place, more than twenty-five years later. To comply with the law, a school must do one of these three things:

- Offer its males and females roughly equal opportunities to play sports. That is, if two thirds of the school's students were male and one third female, then one third of the varsity athletic spots should go to women.

- Show a history of improving opportunities for girls and women.
- Show that it was meeting the demands and interests of its female students. The actual money spent on males and females wouldn't matter—except in scholarship money. If women were about half the athletes, then they should get about half the athletic scholarship money.

More than seven years after Congress passed Title IX, girls and women were surging into new areas and onto new playing fields, and schools had specific guidelines to go by. Title IX was finally taking off. Some of the law's staunchest supporters even began to move on to other women's issues, like the ERA, that needed more attention.

That didn't last long. By the early 1980s, as the country was growing increasingly more conservative, Title IX would face its greatest threat yet— from an unexpected source.

Title IX would face its
greatest threat yet . . .

Right: An editorial cartoon by H. Clay Bennett in the *St. Petersburg Times*.

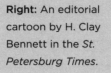

chapter 9

time-out

"I took Title IX for granted."
—Cheryl Miller, college basketball star, 1984

By 1980 political winds were shifting across the country. Taxes were high, the number of people without work was rising, and the economy was stumbling.

Two decades of social change had brought many new opportunities for minorities and women. But they had also led to increased government oversight, and schools, businesses, and average citizens were beginning to complain that the government was meddling much too much in their affairs.

Looking for relief, voters swept Ronald Reagan into the White House and sent a number of conservative politicians to Congress. An engaging speaker and former actor, the new president promised conservative solutions, including slashing social programs, cutting taxes, and hacking away at the thicket of regulations. Tax money, Mr. Reagan told Congress in early 1981, "must not be used to regulate the economy or bring about social change. We've tried that, and surely we must be able to see that it doesn't work."

One area targeted for review—and possible elimination—was Title IX and its athletic rules. In the summer

ELEVATORS

JOB
OPPORTUNITIES
107th FLOOR

H. CLAY BENNETT
Courtesy St. Petersburg Times

Above: An editorial cartoon by H. Clay Bennett in 1988.

of 1981, Vice President George H. W. Bush announced that the Reagan administration had come to believe that Title IX's sports regulations were too burdensome, particularly in requiring that male and female coaches be paid the same and that both sexes get the same amount of sports equipment.

Before the president and his cabinet could actually make changes, another threat to Title IX emerged. Grove City College, a small Pennsylvania school, asked the federal courts to agree that it didn't have to follow the Title IX rules.

In the checks-and-balances system of the U.S. government, the American courts assure that the laws that Congress passes and the rules that government agencies issue are consistent with the U.S. Constitution and applied fairly. One way a person or institution can challenge a law like Title IX is to file a lawsuit.

Grove City's lawsuit dated back to Joseph Califano's efforts to clean up HEW's Title IX files. Mr. Califano had sent every school district and university a new form to sign, promising it would obey Title IX. He viewed the form as "mostly symbolic," proof that HEW was trying to enforce the law. Those that didn't sign would lose their federal funding.

Almost all of the nation's nearly twenty thousand school districts and universities returned their forms. But twenty-two colleges and school districts refused to sign. One of those was Grove City.

Charles MacKenzie, president of Grove City, a fiercely independent Christian college, saw the form as more than symbolic. If he signed it, he believed, the government could potentially have a say in his school's admissions, dormitories, or any other part of college life. That, he said, "would be tantamount to turning over control of the college's future to the federal government."

Grove City College wanted no part of any government interference. It didn't discriminate against any of its 2,200 students. And it went out of its way to avoid taking government money so it wouldn't have to answer to any government agencies. But because Grove City students received some government loans and grants to help them pay tuition, HEW believed the school should sign the form or lose its federal money.

With its students facing the prospect of losing their tuition money, Grove City and four of its students sued HEW in federal court in Pittsburgh.

As the case moved through the legal system Title IX was approaching its tenth anniversary. The progress in just one short decade was amazing. Women comprised one third or more of all law, medical, and veterinary students. In high schools nearly 1.8 million girls were now playing sports, making them one third of all athletes. More than ten thousand women now attended college on athletic scholarships. After Sally Ride became the first woman in space in 1983, the possibilities for females seemed truly limitless. No longer would females accept "No Girls Allowed" attitudes.

Participating, though, was just part of the battle. Girls and women still faced enormous obstacles. Some science teachers and engineering professors were rude to and resentful of the females in their classes, fearing they would drag down their standards. Female sports programs were still second-class, with short seasons, inexperienced and poorly paid coaches, shabby fields, and second-hand equipment.

Dorothy "Dot" Richardson was one of those talented enough to land scholarship money to play softball at UCLA, which had become a standout in women's sports. But the differences between men's and women's sports there were striking. The baseball team would soon play in the brand-new Jackie Robinson Stadium, with fan seating, a press box, and a snack stand. The softball field, by contrast, was hidden among trees, with only two small bleachers. There was no fence, no scoreboard, no locker room. Each player got one glove and a pair of cleats to go with her donated yellow uniform.

At the time that seemed like enough. "To me, it didn't matter,"

No longer would females accept
"No Girls Allowed" attitudes.

Dr. Richardson remembered. "When you've been denied an opportunity and all of a sudden you are getting it, you don't care."

But that opportunity could quickly disappear again, as many athletes were about to learn.

In 1982, Grove City appealed its case to the highest court in the land, the U.S. Supreme Court. Each year the Supreme Court is asked to consider thousands of cases. It agrees to hear only about one hundred—and it agreed to hear the Grove City College case.

Under the Nixon, Ford, and Carter administrations, a school that got any federal money at all had to comply with all federal laws in each of its programs. But in 1983 the Reagan administration and its lawyers at the U.S. Department of Justice changed that long-standing position, just as the Grove City case was about to go before the Supreme Court. Brad Reynolds, a key Justice Department lawyer and the father of five daughters and a son, concluded Title IX had been interpreted incorrectly by regulators. As he read the law, Title IX

applied only to the programs that directly received government money and not to the college or university as a whole. If that was the case, any dormitory, academic department, or sports programs that didn't receive government money could treat males and females differently.

The interpretation by Mr. Reynolds and his colleagues dismayed Title IX supporters and even those inside President Reagan's cabinet. Terrel H. Bell, a longtime educator, was President Reagan's secretary of the Department of Education, a new department that had been split off from HEW. To him, Title IX was helping to end discrimination against women in legal, engineering, and industrial fields, and he read the law to apply to a whole school.

Dr. Bell thought that applying the law only to programs that directly received federal money would harm American education and possibly hurt women and minorities. He also worried that it would be an administrative nightmare, since his department would have to trace where

Below: A "Tank McNamara" cartoon in 1982.

THE NEWSPAPER IS ACTUALLY GOING TO DO AN **ARTICLE** ON THE TEAM!?! PEGGY, YOU'RE **WONDERFUL**!!

WOMEN'S BASKETBALL COACH

JANE, I'LL BE HONEST WITH AS LITTLE INTEREST AS THE SPORTS DESK HAS IN WOMEN'S ATHLETICS, I HAD TO GRAB WHAT COVERAGE I COULD.

THE REPORTER'S FROM THE, UH... 'LIVING TODAY' SECTION...

WELL! PEGGY TELLS ME YOU GUYS SEW YOUR OWN UNIFORMS!

player profile

Dads, Cheerleaders for Their Daughters

Congress passed the law that opened doors for girls and women in school and sports, and the government was charged with enforcing it. But the secret weapons in the fight for fairness were dads.

The generation of girls born in the 1970s and beyond grew up with fathers who firmly believed their girls should have the same experiences as their boys. When teams were dropped, when fields were in disrepair, when the coaching wasn't very good, dads went to bat for their daughters. They protested to principals and school superintendents and sometimes filed the lawsuits that ultimately got girls spots on teams.

Billie Jean King says that men in their forties and fifties still come up to her today to say that they watched her play Bobby Riggs and that the match changed their lives—especially their attitudes about their daughters. "They're the first generation to insist that their daughters and sons have equal opportunities," she said.

Lisa Fernandez, a softball superstar who helped pitch the U.S. team to three Olympic gold medals, said her father encouraged her all the way. As an immigrant from Cuba, he couldn't have known many female athletes growing up. But he urged her to get stronger and to play hard. "I can't say enough about my dad and the support he's always had for me," she said.

every federal dollar went. He felt so strongly about the issue that he took the extraordinary step of asking President Reagan to hear both sides and reconsider.

When Dr. Bell arrived at the White House for the meeting, however, he was told that the president was tied up with pressing matters and wouldn't be there. Instead, a top Reagan aide, Ed Meese, would mediate between Dr. Bell and the Justice Department. Dr. Bell presented a detailed case but to no avail. The administration went ahead with its new interpretation.

Many in Congress were alarmed as well. The House of Representatives, in a very unusual step, passed a resolution by an overwhelming 414–8 vote, insisting that Title IX should apply to all the programs at a school. Fifty members of Congress, including the prominent senator Robert Dole, filed a brief with the Supreme Court, saying that the Reagan administration's position went against the will of Congress. Women's groups and civil rights organizations also protested the Reagan administration's position.

The Supreme Court shocked them all. In a 6-to-3 vote in February 1984 the Court ruled that Title IX applied only to programs directly receiving federal money. Yes, Grove City received government money and would have to sign the form if its students got federal financial aid. But the law applied only to the specific program getting the money—in this case, Grove City's admissions office.

The ruling had a huge impact on American citizens. Title IX was written with the same words as laws banning racial bias and discrimination against the handicapped and older Americans. After the decision the Reagan administration concluded that all of the nation's civil rights laws now applied just as narrowly as Title IX.

Almost immediately, investigations into discrimination were halted. Although the Education Department had found that the University of Mary-land and the University of Washington discriminated against female athletes, both cases were dropped after the Supreme Court decision.

The fight over whether Grove City should fill out a form had left a generation of civil rights laws in tatters. Many senators and representatives pledged to quickly pass a new law restoring what Congress intended. Just three months after the Supreme Court ruling, the House overwhelmingly passed such a bill.

Washington got a strong message about Title IX that autumn from a group of female Olympic medalists. Barely a month after the Los Angeles Olympics, Donna de Varona helped organize a day-long demonstration of

Below: Secretary of Education Terrel H. Bell in the early 1980s.

instant replay

A National Soccer Team

For years after high schools and colleges began adding women's soccer teams, the U.S. Soccer Federation resisted forming a national women's team. When the United States was invited to play in an international women's tournament in the summer of 1985, there was no team to send.

U.S. Soccer Federation officials quickly cobbled together a team and a coach from an Olympics summer sports festival for promising athletes and told them they would be traveling to Italy.

They had three days to practice. There was no budget, but the soccer federation came up with enough money for airfare, a bus, and $10 a day in meal money for each player.

There were no uniforms, either. Just before the team was to leave, it received boxes full of shorts, shirts, and sweat suits—in men's sizes. When the players put them on, "everything came around their ankles," said the coach, Mike Ryan. "They looked like little gorillas walking around." Team members doubled as tailors, staying up well into the night trimming and hemming to bring the uniforms down to size.

The fledgling team tied one game and lost two games in its first tournament. Despite the rocky start, the groundwork was set. In 1991 the women's national team won the first Women's World Cup competition.

support for the bill working its way through Congress. The timing seemed good: Female athletes had made a huge splash in the hometown games, winning twenty-six gold medals and fifty-nine medals overall, more than American women had ever won before. So many female athletes became household names—including runner Mary Decker, petite gold-medal gymnast Mary Lou Retton, and volleyball standout Flo Hyman—that The Washington Post declared, "No longer will Olympic women be exclusively consigned to the deep pages of a sports section. The Games of Los Angeles have given them prominence equal to men."

In September 1984, Ms. Hyman, Ms. Decker, and basketball gold medalist Cheryl Miller traveled to Washington to speak at a breakfast, give interviews with prominent newspapers, and visit senators and representatives, pointing out that Title IX helped make them champions. In fact, most of the women who competed in the 1984 Olympic Games played sports in a college program that probably didn't exist in 1972. "At a critical time in my life," Ms. Hyman said, Title IX "enabled me to receive a scholarship."

In debates senators supporting the bill tried to remind their colleagues of the time before Title IX. Ted Stevens of Alaska told the Senate

Left: President Ronald Reagan and Donna de Varona at a Women's Sports Foundation event in 1983. Ms. de Varona said she invited the president in hopes of making him more aware of the challenges faced by female athletes.

out amid political maneuvering and died without Senate approval.

Without a new law, women, minorities, and the handicapped could no longer call on the federal government for help. Complaints from handicapped students that they couldn't get into some dorms fell by the wayside. A black New Jersey high school student was denied an invitation to the National Honor Society, even though she was near the top of her class. She asked for the government to step in, but the Education Department declined because the program didn't receive any federal funds.

Hundreds of cases were slammed shut. Some students were able to protest under state laws or look to other federal laws for support. Determined, girls continued to play and break down barriers, though sometimes they were rewarded with angry and hostile responses.

that Ms. de Varona had to quit swimming because there weren't athletic scholarships for women. She "is living testimony to the situation that faced women athletes," he said. Dozens of senators agreed with him and backed a restoration bill. But the bill stalled

Hundreds of cases were
slammed shut . . .

Elizabeth Balsley, a fifteen year old from Clinton, New Jersey, wanted a chance to play for her high school's junior varsity football team in 1985, and had to go to court to win the chance to try out. She got more attention from reporters than from her coaches and teammates, and saw little action on the field. Coaches didn't spare their words in describing her shortcomings. "She has no athletic ability whatsoever," the head coach told reporters. "She could work until the cows come home, but she would never be able to play our level of football."

Erin Whitten began playing on boys' hockey teams when she was nine. She tried out for her Glen Falls, New York, high school boys' team because there was no girls' team. After passing a special strength and endurance test—which wasn't required

scorecard 1981–82

High school	1971–72	1981–82
Boys in varsity sports	3,666,917	3,409,081
Girls in varsity sports	294,015	1,810,671
Boys playing football	932,691	927,666
Girls playing volleyball	17,952	282,651
Boys playing basketball	645,670	538,670
Girls playing basketball	132,299	415,381
Boys playing baseball	400,906	415,353
Girls playing softball	9,813	183,176
Boys playing soccer	78,510	161,167
Girls playing soccer	700	51,869
Boys in track and field	642,639	477,650
Girls in track and field	62,211	357,414

College	1971–72	1981–82
Men in college sports	170,384	156,131
Women in college sports	29,977	68,062
Bachelor's degrees awarded to men	500,590	473,364
Bachelor's degrees awarded to women	386,683	479,634
Men entering medical schools	10,435	11,547
Women entering medical schools	1,653	5,113
Men in law schools	85,554	82,410
Women in law schools	8,914	44,902
Men in veterinary schools	5,158	5,026
Women in veterinary schools	702	3,624

of the boys—she became one of the goalies. Her dressing room was in the rink's office.

While Erin's teammates and local fans were supportive, fans of opposing teams sometimes were relentless, jeering and calling her crude names. In a crucial play-off game, spectators sitting behind the goal threw quarters and tampons at her. She simply swept them into the net. Under the circumstances, she could "either accept it or take offense," she said. She laughed it off—and stuck with the sport she loved. (After playing for the University of New Hampshire's women's team, she played in hockey's minor leagues, becoming the first woman goalie to record a win in a men's professional hockey game.)

Without Title IX fully in place, many supporters worried that progress would grind to a halt. Congress tried again to pass a replacement law in 1985 and 1986, but the effort knotted up once more in political issues. Finally, in 1988, after lawmakers agreed to a compromise, the Civil Rights Restoration Act passed Congress.

President Reagan, however, saw the new law as a "big-government power grab." He exercised his presidential power to veto the bill to keep it from becoming law.

After four years of battles Congress was ready to respond. More than two thirds of the members of both the House and the Senate voted to override the veto, allowing the bill to become a law. House Speaker Jim Wright of Texas declared the new law "a step forward in making America truly a land of equal opportunity for all."

A child who had begun first grade just after Title IX was passed was now old enough to have completed high school and graduated from college. In

*Her dressing room
was in the the rink's office.*

player profile

Sally Ride, the First Female Astronaut

Growing up, Sally Ride had two loves, tennis and science—so much so that she had her own subscription to *Scientific American*. Still, she set off to college in 1968 to play tennis, not to conquer the mysteries of space.

For a time, she even tried to play tennis full-time but quickly decided that science was more practical. While she competed for the Stanford University tennis team, she earned an undergraduate degree in physics in 1973. She received her Ph.D. in 1978.

She was preparing to become a research scientist when an ad in the Stanford newspaper caught her eye: The National Aeronautics and Space Administration (NASA) was looking for astronauts, particularly women. She applied and was accepted.

In NASA's program her tennis experience paid off. She knew about teamwork, focus, and how to channel her competitive energy. Those skills came in handy when she was chosen to fly a 1983 space shuttle mission, becoming the first woman in space.

She trained carefully, realizing that she had to know her job perfectly so that no one would doubt that she belonged there. Much as her tennis idol Billie Jean King learned when she played Bobby Riggs, Ms. Ride realized, "I just couldn't make any mistakes." She didn't, and she gained worldwide fame for her two successful missions.

Today, she has turned her attention to encouraging middle school girls to explore science, math, and technology. Through her company Imaginary Lines, she has offered camps and one-day science festivals to draw girls in, knowing that far more girls than boys drift away from science and math in middle school. While girls today have far more opportunities than before, she says, in many schools "it's still not cool to be the best one in the math class."

player profile

Edith Green, 1910–1987

In her retirement years Edith Green continued to crusade. She endorsed political candidates, pushed for a senior citizens' center, and lobbied intensely for a new shelter in downtown Portland for homeless teens, which was aptly named "Greenhouse."

Though she had been controversial, her former colleagues in Congress remembered her determination and her many accomplishments. Mrs. Green "did not suffer fools gladly—including this one," wrote the esteemed New York senator Daniel Patrick Moynihan when she retired. But, he added, "she presided over the enactment of the most important education legislation in the history of the Republic, and I would hope someone would say so."

When she looked back in her final years, Mrs. Green remained most proud of her efforts to expand educational opportunities for all, and to create new possibilities for girls and women, especially through Title IX. Her greatest satisfaction in her work had come in spending months or years on a law and watching it take effect.

Legislation "has the potential of literally affecting the lives of millions of people in the years ahead," she said. "I think that is really a great reward—that I have played at least a small part in making opportunities available to others that were never available before."

Edith Green died of cancer in April 1987 at the age of seventy-seven.

the sixteen years since the law was passed, the government's commitment and enforcement had waxed and waned and legislators had fiercely debated every point. But every time the issue came to a decisive vote, the United State Congress stood solidly behind its law to stop sex discrimination in schools. Despite Title IX's ups and downs, its goals were now woven into the fabric of America's culture.

Young men and women hardly knew a time when girls and boys didn't compete in nearly every area of education. With Title IX restored, refurbished, and stronger than ever, the payoff was finally near.

comeback

"The eighties you can bury as far as I'm concerned. The nineties were like a renaissance."

—Christine H.B. Grant, long-time women's athletic director at the University of Iowa

Below: A "Peanuts" cartoon in 1990.

The last decade of the twentieth century began with a bombshell for women's sports. As women's teams began to gather in Knoxville, Tennessee, for the 1990 Women's Final Four basketball championship, the University of Oklahoma, long a

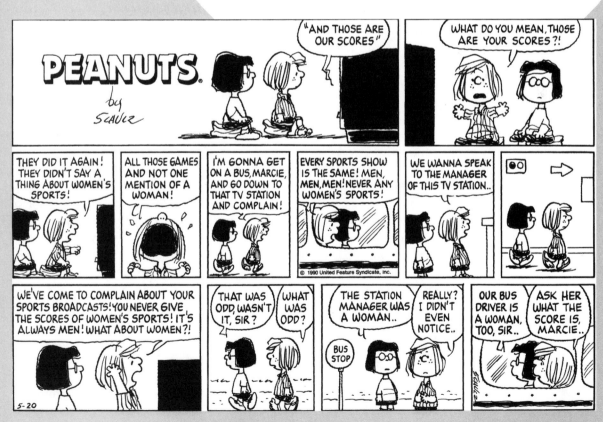

Above: A 1992 "Doonesbury" cartoon responds to research that boys get more attention in the classroom than girls do.

force in football and men's basketball, announced it was killing its women's basketball program.

Basketball had become the most popular and successful of the women's sports, and nearly every major college had a women's team. But Oklahoma's team had turned in two losing seasons and was drawing a pathetic sixty-five spectators to each game. The men's basketball coach called funding for the team "money down the drain."

Oklahoma athletic officials decided that the $300,000 a year spent on women's basketball could be better spent on other existing women's teams. The players believed the problem wasn't the team, but an apathetic university administration. Their coaching was lacking, and when they asked for money to advertise their games, an official encouraged them to sell cookies or hold a raffle.

In past years the fury over shutting down the team might have died there, just another dispute in the "Briefly Noted" column of the sports pages. Now, though, too much had changed. Too much was expected by and for women. This was national news.

Other college women's basketball coaches denounced the move. A Washington, D.C., lawyer, experienced in Title IX cases, threatened a lawsuit.

The Oklahoma governor shrugged at the decision, saying, "It doesn't bother me." But other state politicians were plenty bothered. The Oklahoma senate quickly passed a resolution condemning the decision. One senator even asked the university to apologize for bringing such embarrassment to the state.

The huge outcry made a difference. Barely a week after abolishing women's basketball, the university reversed its call and agreed to build up the team, citing an "outpouring of support" from all around the state.

The Oklahoma flip-flop underscored the changing views of female athletes and girls and women in general. More women than ever were working, and they were gradually moving into positions of power in companies, schools, and government. Hard work in the classroom and on the playing field was bringing females respect and melting away many old attitudes.

In fact, old-fashioned views about girls—ones that had simply been accepted in the 1960s—now were harshly criticized. A 1992 report from the American Association of University Women looked at more than one thousand studies of girls in the classroom and found that boys' expectations were built up while girls' were whittled back. Many science teachers and some math teachers ignored girls in favor of boys. Teachers tended to call on boys more often and help them with reading far more than they helped girls with math. Boys were allowed to yell out answers, whereas girls who spoke out of turn were scolded.

While the boys seemed to have a part in everything, Jennie Montour, an eleven year old from St. Paul,

scorecard 1991–92

High-school	1971–72	1991–92
Boys in varsity sports	3,666,917	3,429,853
Girls in varsity sports	294,015	1,940,801
Boys playing football	932,691	912,845
Girls playing volleyball	17,952	293,948
Boys playing basketball	645,670	518,127
Girls playing basketball	132,299	391,612
Boys playing baseball	400,906	433,684
Girls playing softball	9,813	221,510
Boys playing soccer	78,510	236,082
Girls playing soccer	700	135,302
Boys in track and field	642,639	417,451
Girls in track and field	62,211	327,183

College	1971–72	1991–92
Men in college sports	170,384	186,047
Women in college sports	29,977	96,469
Men entering medical schools	10,435	9,778
Women entering medical schools	1,653	6,433
Men in law schools	85,554	78,152
Women in law schools	8,914	57,005
Men in veterinary schools	5,158	3,647
Women in veterinary schools	702	6,044

player profile

Amy Cohen, Challenging Brown University

Amy Cohen had never heard of Title IX when Brown University announced it would no longer fund her gymnastics team. All she wanted was a chance to compete in her senior year.

Assured that they could compete if they raised enough money, the teammates went to work. Gymnasts did backflips on the lawn for quarters. Teams from competing schools sent small donations and let them help at a clinic. Teammates called parents and alumni seeking help. To defray costs, they sewed their own practice leotards.

Even with some money in hand, the gymnasts were barred from competing as a varsity team. They weren't allowed in the varsity locker room or in the weight room.

Their complaint to the university turned into a lawsuit. Friends questioned why Amy was challenging Brown. "People said, 'Don't you think a big institution would know better than you? Don't you think they have good legal advice?'" she said. Both men and women athletes were afraid to speak up initially for fear that their sports would lose funding too.

Ms. Cohen was surprised to see *Cohen v. Brown* go on and on. It ultimately ended when the Supreme Court refused to hear Brown's appeal of a ruling that found it had violated Title IX. As a result, Brown had to reinstate gymnastics and look for more ways to support women athletes. The decision forced other universities to examine their own programs.

"I didn't start out and say, Title IX is what is really important to me and equality for women is really important to me. It sort of became that way," said Ms. Cohen, now a schoolteacher. "I'm very proud of what we did."

Minnesota, told *Newsweek*, her teachers made her feel "that I was stupid."

Even though girls got better grades than boys and were more likely to go to college, the study found they had less confidence in their abilities and more modest goals. As a result, they were less likely to reach their true potential. The report created a furor, prompting teachers and parents to pay closer attention to young women.

On the athletics front, the National Federation of State High School Associations reported that girls now had many more sports teams than before. But boys' teams were likely to have assistant coaches; girls' teams were not. Boys often got new uniforms every year; girls got them every three years. Boys had junior varsity teams; girls did not.

The NCAA, which had battled Title IX so long and hard in the 1970s and early 1980s, became an advocate for women. Under executive director

Richard D. Schultz, the organization took its first close look at how female athletes were faring—and the picture wasn't particularly flattering. As Title IX turned twenty years old, only twenty-three cents of every college sports dollar was spent on women's teams. About three of every ten varsity athletes were female, though more than half the nation's college students were women.

Mr. Schultz believed the NCAA could do more to encourage more women to play. "We must be pro-active, we must be a leader," he said. "This is more than a financial issue. It's a moral issue as well."

The culture shift came with a renewed recognition of a rejuvenated Title IX—and a surge of lawsuits. The government hadn't pursued Title IX cases aggressively, so girls and women took the law into their own hands. In 1991, Brown University eliminated two women's sports, volleyball and gymnastics, and two men's sports, water polo and golf, in a budget-cutting move. Unable to change the athletic director's mind, gymnastics team members consulted a lawyer familiar with Title IX.

From Brown's point of view, there wasn't a problem. It offered more women's sports than most schools,

with sixteen teams to fifteen men's teams. It considered itself a model of equality. If it wasn't fair to women, it figured, no one was.

As a lawsuit moved forward, the gymnasts' lawyers uncovered one shortcoming after another. The women's field hockey and lacrosse teams shared uniforms; men's teams didn't have to share. The women's ice hockey team got a limited number of sticks; the men, unlimited sticks. Women's locker rooms were spare and crowded. Every Brown athlete, from gymnasts to football players, got the same workout clothes—in men's size large or extra-large. The lawyers even got down to bare-bones details, pointing out that men got university-issued athletic supporters. Women had to buy their own athletic bras.

In time Brown settled part of the suit, fixing up the women's locker rooms, adding better equipment, and even buying athletic bras. But the Providence, Rhode Island, university continued to argue that it met the standards of Title IX.

The courts disagreed. After a long battle an appeals court in 1996 ruled that Brown hadn't met any of the three tests for Title IX set out in 1979. While women were nearly half of Brown's students, the court said, they

It's a *moral issue.*

were just over one third of the athletes and got just one quarter of the dollars spent on varsity sports. Brown didn't meet the first test for Title IX because women's participation didn't reflect the percentage of women students at Brown.

Under the second test, the court said, Brown hadn't added or built up a women's team in a decade, so it couldn't show that it was working to improve opportunities for women. Brown argued that it met the third test, meeting women's interests with its programs, because females simply were not as interested in sports as males.

Brown noted that far fewer women than men played on its intramural sports teams. At the time, just under five percent of female high-school athletes went on to play varsity college sports, while a little more than five percent of male high-school athletes competed at the college level. To Brown—and many others—the reason was that fewer women wanted to play.

But the court saw the argument differently. The judges concluded that

without a chance to play and without teams to play on, women couldn't compete. Brown had eliminated two successful teams, so obviously those women had been interested. Furthermore, the court said, the Title IX rules were meant to go beyond stereotypes and to recognize that "women's lower rate of participation in athletics reflects women's historical lack of opportunities to participate in sports."

The 1996 court ruling caught Brown and many other schools by surprise. The court was telling schools that just offering women's sports wasn't enough. Schools had to pay attention to the quantity and quality of their teams, their coaching, their equipment, their locker rooms. With the courts sending a clear message that Title IX was alive and well, schools began to review and add girls' and women's teams again.

If schools needed more proof that females were truly serious about sports, they got it in Atlanta in 1996. Male athletes may shine on professional teams, but women strut their stuff at the Olympic Games. About 3,800 women would compete in

Below: A Greg Howard "Sally Forth" cartoon in 1991.

these Summer Games, about 1,100 more than in 1992.

The female athletes of the mid-1990s were a different breed than those who competed before them. Most were born in the early 1970s and grew up with access to leagues and teams that their mothers had only dreamed about. Dubbed "Title IX babies," many of the team sports players had attended college on athletic scholarships or at least had gotten to play on college teams. And in this Olympic year the United States, the host country, was committed to their success.

Disappointed by a third-place finish in 1992, USA Basketball spent $3 million to allow the women's national team to train and tour together for the better part of a year since women didn't have a professional league like the men did. Tara VanDerveer took a leave from her job as the women's basketball coach at Stanford University to mold a team out of current and former college players. Some of them hadn't played competitively in a long time. College star Sheryl Swoopes had been working as a bank teller in west Texas and playing pickup ball at a recreation center while waiting for a chance to compete in the Olympics.

In softball Dot Richardson had struggled to balance her dreams of

player profile

Mia Hamm, Soccer Superstar

Soccer superstar Mia Hamm has watched interest in women's sports and in soccer grow almost side by side.

Athletic from the time she was tiny, she began playing soccer at the age of five on teams consisting mostly of boys and joined a boys' team for eleven-year-olds when she was just ten. In seventh grade she even played a season of junior high football.

Growing up, she didn't have girls' teams to play on or women's teams to watch on television. She joined her first all-girl soccer team at eleven and was playing on the nascent women's national team by the time she was fifteen. Funding was so tight that the team took vans to their games, with the older players sometimes doing the driving.

The team brought home the first Women's World Cup in 1991, but hardly anyone heard about it. By the 1999 World Cup competition, though, strangers in airports were wishing the team good luck. One day NBC news anchor Tom Brokaw showed up during a practice—the ultimate evidence that women's soccer had hit the big time. The sold-out crowds only reaffirmed the team's stature.

For Ms. Hamm, the real value of Title IX was the chance to land a scholarship to the University of North Carolina. Without it, she said, she wouldn't have been able to attend a four-year university. Athletics gave her an education, as well as skills and self-esteem.

Through a foundation she set up after the 1999 World Cup, she hopes to help give young women more options in athletics. "My life has taken the path it has because of sports," she said. "But we need to continue to push forward and make sure we get girls as many opportunities as possible."

becoming a doctor and playing at a world-class level. During her second year of medical school, she split her time between schoolwork and preparing for national-team tryouts—and failed her year-end exams. She had to repeat the year. This time she rededicated herself to her studies while making sacrifices in softball, ultimately earning her degree and beginning a residency in orthopedic surgery. But in 1996, with softball making its Olympic debut, she turned her attention back to her first love. The hospital allowed her to take a year off to practice and train.

All the women's teams promised to be competitive. But the NBC television network figured viewers wanted to see the glamour sports, like men's basketball, women's gymnastics, swimming, diving, and track,

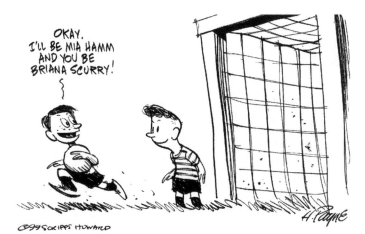

Above: A Henry Payne editorial cartoon for Scripps Howard newspapers.

during the prime evening hours. Women's soccer and basketball would be shown in the off-hours or late at night. Women's softball wasn't on the schedule at all, and only the highlights, not the games, were broadcast.

Even without the television cameras, the women brought out fans in record numbers. The softball team sold out every game as it swept through the competition to capture the gold medal.

Dr. Richardson, now thirty-four years old, had dreamed of hitting home runs in the Olympics, and she blasted off several, including a two-run shot in the gold-medal game against China.

Her energy and enthusiasm in postgame interviews were contagious, and she quickly became a national star. Dr. Richardson was supposed to get back to work at the hospital job two days after the final game. But Olympic fever was so high that after a rousing welcome-home celebration, the hospital gave her a second week off to go to Disney World and the White House and to hit some pitches in the middle of Manhattan on the *Late Show With David Letterman*.

Women's soccer, also appearing for the first time in the Olympics, filled a 76,000-seat stadium, introducing eager fans to Mia Hamm, Brandi Chastain, and Brianna Scurry. They won another gold medal.

The Olympic basketball team drew more than 30,000 spectators to the Georgia Dome. Coach VanDerveer was awed by the power of her players and their supporters as the team scored more than 100 points in the championship game to defeat the previous world champion, Brazil. As she watched the celebration she couldn't help but remember her days as a school mascot in a bear suit. Her team had just won a gold medal in a sport she hadn't been allowed to play in junior high!

The victory didn't belong just to a small group of athletes, she realized, but to all the people who had worked to make basketball possible for them. "It was not only a year of grueling workouts and exhausting travel," she wrote later, "but decades of women—and men—selling cupcakes to buy uniforms, hounding athletic directors for scholarships, refusing to accept

Above: U.S. Olympic women's hockey team goalie, Sarah Tueting, waves, and her teammates respond to cheering fans after the team beat Canada to win the gold medal in 1998.

second-class status, believing in the game and in women when there wasn't even a national tournament, much less an Olympic one."

When the games were over, the women had won gold in an amazing array of sports: swimming, track and field, gymnastics, soccer, synchronized swimming, basketball, and softball. Their heart-pounding success refocused attention on the incredible gains women had made.

Christine H. B. Grant, longtime women's athletic director at the University of Iowa, had spent her career trying to sell the benefits of women's sports. She was astounded—and thrilled—to be turned away from some women's events because the tickets were sold out. She did manage to get into a semifinal soccer game that went into overtime. Amid a screaming, sellout crowd, the magni-

tude of the event hit her. For the first time, she said, "it struck me what women had done. And what women had done was change the society forever." It was, she thought, "a miracle."

The nation's young women weren't finished. The U.S. women's hockey team was made up of players who often had to play on boys' teams, players who had grown up slapping away criticism that girls didn't belong in such a down-and-dirty "male" sport. In the Winter Olympics in 1998 the women outmuscled the world competition and ended up in the gold-medal game against their toughest rival, Canada. When the U.S. women won, even hard-boiled sportswriters had to wipe tears away. "This was a triumph for anyone, male or female, whose dream has ever been ridiculed," wrote one.

General Mills chose the team for the celebrated spot on its Wheaties box. "That stretching sound you hear," wrote *Sports Illustrated,* "is attitudes about women athletes continuing to expand."

The expansion would continue to swell to worldly proportions in 1999, when the U.S. women's soccer team pursued the Women's World Cup, soccer's most prestigious triumph. The U.S. men had trouble competing

in the every-four-years competition against powerhouses from Latin America and Europe. But the women's game was new, and the U.S. women were among the best.

When the women's national team brought home the very first Women's World Cup from China in 1991, star forward Mia Hamm remembered that only a few family and close friends greeted them at the airport.

In 1995 the team lost in the semifinals to Norway. But the 1999 World Cup, played in mammoth stadiums in the United States, brought in tens of thousands of fans, many of

them soccer-playing youngsters. As the U.S. women convincingly marched through the three-week competition, beating Denmark, England, and Italy, the game stories and the attention moved from the back of sports pages to the front page.

On July 10 the women faced China in the championship game. A crowd of more than ninety thousand people gathered to watch, the largest crowd ever at a women's sporting event. Girls and boys with painted faces and American flags, some sporting jerseys with Mia Hamm's number 9, filled the seats. More than forty million people

scorecard 1996–97

Degrees awarded to women	1971-72	1996-97
Business	11,578	110,096
Law	1,498	17,531
Medicine	830	6,450
Dentistry	43	1,397
Computer Science	461	6,731
Engineering	526	12,491

Why Brandi Chastain and the U.S. Women's Soccer Team Were Unbeatable

JULY 19, 1999
www.cnnsi.com

Above:

Sports Illustrated celebrated the success of the American women in the Women's World Cup in 1999.

watched on television as the United States and China battled to a 0–0 tie.

No one scored in two overtimes, sending the game to a penalty-kick shoot-out. Five players from each team would get a shot at the goal, a one-on-one face-off between kicker and goalie. The USA matched China kick for kick, until U.S. goalie Briana Scurry blocked China's third shot.

Brandi Chastain booted America's fifth kick into the net, giving the United States the victory. In ecstatic celebration, she stripped off her shirt—"momentary insanity," she said later—proudly displaying the muscle and confidence that seemed to define the whole team. The crowd roared,

and the millions watching on television cheered with them.

One of the proudest spectators was Donna de Varona. As chairwoman of the World Cup, she had helped market the games and fill the stadiums. Her dad had played in this same stadium before a sold-out crowd in the 1938 Rose Bowl. Now women were the stars—so much so that her young son was swept away by the excitement. "Mom," he asked, "do you think they'll ever do that for men?"

The once little-known women soccer players were now as famous as any Hollywood celebrity. They gave endless interviews for television and appeared on a stream of magazine covers. FLAT-OUT FANTASTIC, *Time* said. GIRLS RULE! screamed the front of *Newsweek*.

As 1999 wrapped up, *Sports Illustrated* named the team "Sportswomen of the Year." They hadn't just won a big trophy, the magazine said. They had raised women's sports to new heights, again elevating the expectations of what females could do. Their win "was the most significant day in the history of women's sports, bearing the fruit of the passage of Title IX in 1972 and surpassing by a long shot that burn-your-bra night

instant replay

A New Meaning for Title IX

After months of trying to fight off a boy in her fifth-grade class in Forsyth, Georgia, LaShonda Davis made clear that she couldn't take his advances anymore. "Do you and Dad have a lawyer?" she finally asked her mom.

For months during the 1992–93 school year, the boy had rubbed up against the ten-year-old, tried to grab her breasts, and made vulgar comments such as, "I want to get in bed with you." Though she had reported the incidents to her teachers, the boy had never been disciplined. In fact, he continued to sit next to her in class for months after her first complaints.

Aurelia Davis, LaShonda's mom, tried talking with the teachers and the principal, but no one seemed to take the behavior seriously. LaShonda's grades dropped, and in the spring her father found a suicide note. Finally, the family went to the sheriff. The boy pleaded guilty to sexual battery in juvenile court.

Frustrated with the school's lack of concern, Mrs. Davis sued the Monroe County Board of Education in 1994. Though sexual harassment wasn't even a concept when Title IX became law, courts had ruled that sexual harassment of students by teachers was sex discrimination that violated Title IX. But what about sexual harassment of one student by another?

Ultimately, the Davis family's request for a trial ended up before the U.S. Supreme Court. In 1999, in a bitterly divided 5-to-4 decision, the high court ruled that the family could sue the school board. When a harasser's "severe and pervasive" behavior hurts a child's ability to learn and the school shows "deliberate indifference," the district can be held accountable, Justice Sandra Day O'Connor wrote.

Dissenters fretted that the case would lead to a flood of lawsuits over all kinds of typical childish behavior. "After today, Johnny will find the routine problems of adolescence are to be resolved by invoking a federal right to demand assignment to a desk two rows away," wrote Justice Anthony Kennedy.

The Davis case never went to trial. The family settled with the school district in 2001, when LaShonda was already in college. The process was tough on the shy young lady, who was uncomfortable with all the media attention. Mrs. Davis said she doesn't know if LaShonda would go through such an ordeal again. But she knows that she would. "To me, it's the right thing to do," Mrs. Davis said. "I did what I had to do as a parent."

instant replay

"If You Let Me Play"

In the mid-1990s the giant shoe company Nike Inc. decided it wanted to show some leadership in helping women in sports. A marketing group sat down to brainstorm.

Title IX had removed the legal barrier, and girls had more opportunities than ever. But society still thought sports were more important for boys than for girls. Girls didn't get much encouragement to play.

The Nike team took that idea, along with research from the Women's Sports Foundation on how sports helps girls, to Nike's ad agency, Wieden & Kennedy. The agency decided to let girls tell the story:

If you let me play sports,
I will like myself more;
I will have more self-confidence
If you let me play sports.

The resulting advertisement, "If You Let Me Play," had even the most cynical viewers choking back tears.

Calls and letters poured in from women young and old, grateful to see such support for girls. The ad won awards, including a Best of Show from the One Club for Art and Copy in New York. Even today, the innocent faces send a powerful message.

in '73 when Billie Jean King beat Bobby Riggs," the magazine gushed. "In the final summer of the 20th century, the era of the woman in sports finally arrived."

Twenty-seven years before, a little-known law called Title IX had provided the muscle to pry open doors for girls and women, and the determination, grit, and perseverance of a generation had carried them over the threshold. Now everyone knew that girls could—and should—play. The only question left was how far their strength, skill, and courage would take them.

epilogue: extra innings

At the 2002 U.S. Open, a reporter interviewing tennis star Jennifer Capriati noted that President George W. Bush was considering changing the rules of Title IX, described as "the legislation that helped get women involved in sports."

"If you could say something to President Bush, what would you say?" the reporter asked.

"I have no idea what Title IX is," Ms. Capriati replied. "Sorry."

—*Associated Press*

The headline about a big basketball game at the top of the Sunday sports section of the *New York Times* in February 2003 read like so many others: NO. 1 DUKE IS NO. 59 IN UCONN'S STREAK. The Huskies of the University of Connecticut had built a big lead against the top-ranked Duke University Blue Devils and held on, winning their fifty-ninth consecutive game. But the picture of three players told a less-than-expected story: This was a battle between the nation's two top-ranked *women's* teams. The newspaper didn't need to tell its readers that. It assumed they already knew.

For some time, the dominating University of Connecticut women's team had drawn sellout crowds at home. This time, for the first time, the Duke women had filled their stadium too. Some students had even camped out for a night or two to guarantee a seat.

In another story the *Times* hailed the significance: "The game reconfirmed that given equal opportunity, determined university support and suitable news media attention, women can provide competition every bit as engaging and remunerative as their counterparts on men's teams," reporter Jere Longman wrote.

Clearly, girls and women had come a long way, both in sports and in schooling in general. In 1972 many

SERENA AND VENUS WILLIAMS, MARION JONES, DOMINIQUE DAWES...

..LISA LESLIE, CATHY FREEMAN, LAILA ALI.

THE NEXT TIME SOMEONE TELLS ME I PLAY LIKE A GIRL...

..I'M GONNA SAY "THANKS".

BENTLEY
© 2004 Creators Syndicate, Inc.

men thought women weren't interested in law or medicine or veterinary work. In the 1970s women didn't apply to professional schools because they knew they would be turned away—or turned down later for jobs. Once the options were available, though, they jumped at them. By 2002 just about half of all U.S. law and medical students were women, as were roughly three of every four veterinary students.

Females are still just a tiny minority of engineering and computer science graduates. But they are the majority on college campuses. The number of female undergraduate students surged in the 1980s and kept growing. Today, women earn about fifty-seven of every one hundred bachelor's degrees—putting them where men were in the early 1970s.

Girls and women nationwide numbered more than four out of every ten high school and college varsity athletes in 2002, well ahead of the early 1990s, though still well below their enrollment on school campuses. Many, but not all, stereotypes have melted away. Athletic girls and their strong, muscular bodies are admired, not criticized. Professional female athletes may face questions about their dating habits, but the most intense focus remains on their skills. Though publicity about her lesbian affair was scandalous in the early 1980s, Billie Jean King, long divorced, is far better known for the impact she has had on women's sports than for being gay.

At the same time, thirty years of progress have also created new and unexpected problems. Once, nearly all women's teams had female coaches. But as women's sports grew in importance and popularity, coaching women became more attractive to men. In the 2001-2002 school year male coaches led 56 percent of college women's teams, the largest number since Title IX was passed. Meanwhile, few women coach men's teams.

Educational differences linger. Overall, girls still aren't pushed to stick with math and science in high school. To change that, Rensselaer Polytechnic Institute tries to introduce girls to

Above: A "Herb & Jamal" cartoon by Stephen Bentley in 2001.

Opposite: Lisa Leslie holds up the 2001 WNBA Championship trophy after leading the Los Angeles Sparks to victory.

player profile

Lisa Leslie, Slam-Dunk Star

Lisa Leslie was a true Title IX baby, born in 1972, the same year the law was passed.

As a kid, she wasn't interested in much more than jumping rope and kickball. But in seventh grade her school offered basketball, volleyball, softball, and track, and she played all four. Had the teams not been there, she said, she might have never played sports at all. But once she tried them, she was hooked.

In eighth grade her new school didn't have a girls' basketball team, so she played in a boys' recreational league. At first, the boys refused to pass to her. That didn't last long. She began stealing the basketball and scoring. "They've been passing to me ever since," she said.

On her high school basketball team in Inglewood, California, in the late 1980s, she was as domineering as Cheryl Miller had been a decade before. One record, though, remained out of reach. In a stunning display of shooting, she scored 101 points in one game—in the first half. With her team leading 102–24, the other team forfeited. Unable to finish the game, Lisa couldn't break Cheryl Miller's game record of 105 points.

Title IX gave Lisa a ticket to college, something her single mother couldn't provide. But she noticed quickly at the University of Southern California that the men's teams got special treatment. For instance, the men's basketball team stayed in hotels before home games and ate every day at a training table bulging with catered food. The women were fed only on game day. For a cash-strapped college student, she remembered, "what kind of meal you get is pretty big."

Since college she has played on three gold-medal Olympic teams and led the Los Angeles Sparks to two Women's National Basketball Association (WNBA) championships. And she broke one of the last basketball barriers, becoming the first woman to dunk in a professional game.

Realizing that Title IX made a difference in her life, she has walked Capitol Hill several times to remind Congress to stand behind it. She knows that around the country little girls are practicing and playing and dreaming that they can someday break Lisa Leslie's records. To her, that's how it should be. "We just want to play," she said. "We shouldn't have to fight for Title IX every year."

Above: A "Tank McNamara" cartoon in 2002.

science and engineering in middle school, before well-meaning adults and social pressures convince them that they aren't good at math. A Senate subcommittee looking at the shortage of women in the physical and computer sciences and engineering learned that girls and women were discouraged in many ways, from their hands-on lab time to a shortage of women teachers as role models.

Some high schools and middle schools have continued to short-change girls' athletic programs. In one New Orleans school the boys' baseball team had its own field, while the girls' softball team practiced on the school's front lawn. In 2001 a federal court ruled that Michigan's high school athletic association discriminated against girls by making them play basketball in the fall instead of the winter, volleyball in the winter instead of the fall, and other sports in nontraditional seasons. The odd schedules meant that college recruiters and those who put together national rankings weren't around when the Michigan girls played, limiting their chances for scholarships. The unusual seasons had been set many years before—so that boys' teams wouldn't be inconvenienced. Reluctantly, the state had to rearrange its schedules.

With more and more female athletes crowding onto formerly male turf and sports budgets growing tighter, Title IX began to generate an emotional backlash not seen since the mid-1970s. That fueled a renewed round of girl-versus-boy debates. To accommodate women as well as expensive football and basketball programs, some schools cut lower-profile men's teams like gymnastics, wrestling, and swimming. Some male athletes and coaches charged that in the rush to provide opportunities for females, schools discriminated against males. Yet many schools continued to spend heavily on football and men's basketball, paying million-dollar coaching salaries and offering special dorms and dining rooms for those athletes.

Those who fought for Title IX encountered a ticklish new territory. Doris Brown Heritage, who worked so hard for the chance to run competitively as a young woman, was a cross-country and track coach for years at

Seattle Pacific University, where there are two female students for every male. To balance out the university's scholarships, women got track scholarships and men didn't.

This wasn't what she had in mind when she was fighting for opportunity herself. "To me, it's really important that we not just rob Peter to pay Paul," Ms. Heritage said. The spirit of the law should be "to look at what's good for people and not what's good for men and what's good for women."

Through careful budgeting and extra fund-raising, most schools added athletic opportunities for women without taking teams from men. But when a men's team was cut back or a whole sport dropped, Title IX was often blamed.

In 2002, St. John's University said it would end its football program, which didn't offer any scholarships. It also cut men's cross-country and track and the men's and women's swimming teams and added a men's lacrosse team. Rev. Donald J. Harrington, president of the Jamaica, New York, school, acknowledged that many observers would conclude the decision was made solely because of Title IX.

It wasn't, he insisted. Rather, it "was done as a matter of justice." With women making up well over half of St. John's students, "it would be very difficult for me to explain to them why their tuition dollars were being used to support athletic programs that were made up of 65 percent men," he said. Even with different Title IX rules, he added, "we still would have made the same decision based on what is just to our students."

Rev. Harrington's stance was a rare one. To many, "Title IX" had become a dirty word. The National Wrestling Coaches Association, frustrated at watching the number of college wrestling teams dwindle, argued that Title IX rules were the culprit and were hurting men. Men are more interested in sports than women, the group said, and are unfairly penalized when schools try to boost the number of women athletes. "It's just illogical to use this one-size-fits-all measurement," said Mike Moyer, executive director of the wrestling coaches' group.

What was done was a
matter of justice.

player profile

Ron Wyden, a New Title IX Advocate

As the chairman of the U.S. Senate's Science and Technology Subcommittee, Senator Ron Wyden of Oregon saw that relatively few women were working in math and technology fields. In fact, in computer sciences the number of women earning degrees was shrinking.

Fearing strong talent was being left behind, he held hearings in 2002 to see if the government could change the trend. Experts testified that girls still face stereotypes in pursuing math and science and that at higher levels of study women run into more obstacles than men.

In one hearing an engineering dean pointed out that enforcing Title IX would help. Mr. Wyden, who had attended college on a basketball scholarship, was confused.

Title IX was a sports law, wasn't it? When he learned the law applied to academics, too, "I just said, 'holy Toledo,' I didn't know this."

He has become a cheerleader for enforcing the law to eliminate bias in schools, universities, and research labs. "I think the biggest problem is just neglect, disinterest, and lack of awareness," he said. The other hurdle is education—making sure people know that Title IX is as relevant to the classroom as it is to the gym.

Mr. Wyden, who once held Edith Green's old congressional seat, now realizes that he is building on her work. Ensuring opportunities for women was "her dream and her hope," he said. "I am now very proud to pick up the torch of Edith Green."

The wrestling group's complaints prompted U.S. Education Secretary Rod Paige to appoint a special commission in 2002 to review "opportunity in athletics." The commission, made up of athletes, athletic directors, and others, including longtime advocate Donna de Varona, held meetings around the country and heard passionate pleas for and against the law. After months of hearings and discussions the commission recommended that the Education Department discourage schools from cutting men's teams or capping how big those teams can be in the name of Title IX. It also questioned whether the department's tests for measuring whether schools comply with Title IX could be improved. That frightened supporters, who feared that the rules might be watered down.

Concerned, Ms. de Varona and soccer star Julie Foudy, another commission member, issued a minority report, disagreeing with the commission's conclusions. Title IX supporters helped organize rallies in Washington. They used e-mail lists and mailings to encourage soccer moms and dads, sports groups, and others to send e-mails and letters backing the law.

On a Friday afternoon in July 2003, the Education Department quietly released a letter saying it would leave Title IX and its rules alone. While it discouraged schools from slashing men's teams to benefit women's sports, it took no other action. Overall, it said, the department "found very broad support throughout the country for the goals and spirit of Title IX." The little law had survived yet another threat.

What happens next will depend more on what girls growing up today do in the classroom and in competition than on anything the government might do. Will girls get the support and backing to take physical science, engineering, and math courses in greater numbers? Will more women move from teaching jobs into principal and administrative positions? Will women crack the coaching barriers to lead more women's teams—or even break into coaching men's teams? How exactly will equal opportunity evolve?

Donna Shalala, president of the University of Miami, believes equal opportunity will be reached "when the men in sports come to the women's games" and when university fans don't "moan and groan" about efforts to improve women's sports. It will happen "when 'Title IX' is not a bad word," she said.

To her, the problem is simpler than the solution. Though Miami has regularly fielded one of the nation's finest football teams, well over half its students are female. Dr. Shalala would like more chances for women to

Below: NCAA President Cedric Dempsey testifies in November 2002 in support of Title IX before Education Secretary Rod Paige's special commission on athletic opportunities.

121

scorecard 2001–02

High-school	1971–72	2001–02
Boys in varsity sports	3,666,917	3,960,517
Girls in varsity sports	294,015	2,806,998
Boys playing football	932,691	1,023,712
Girls playing volleyball	17,952	395,124
Boys playing basketball	645,670	540,597
Girls playing basketball	132,299	456,169
Boys playing baseball	400,906	451,674
Girls playing softball	9,813	355,960
Boys playing soccer	78,510	339,101
Girls playing soccer	700	295,265
Boys in track and field	642,639	494,022
Girls in track and field	62,211	415,677

College	1971–72	2001–02
Men in college sports	170,384	212,140
Women in college sports	29,977	155,513
Bachelor's degrees awarded to men	500,590	538,000
Bachelor's degrees awarded to women	386,683	744,000
Men entering medical schools	10,435	8,581
Women entering medical schools	1,653	7,784
Men in law schools	85,554	69,390
Women in law schools	8,914	65,701

play sports—and she would also like to see more men applying for admission. "Title IX is as much about young men as it is about young women," she said. "It's about everybody having the same opportunity."

Norma Cantú, a former assistant secretary of education and now a law professor, has another perspective. In most sports, she noted, teams switch sides at the halfway point. If the court is flawed or the wind is blowing a certain way, each team has to deal with the problem. "The job of Title IX will be done when one group will willingly trade places with the other group," she said.

That time hasn't come yet. For the most part, male players on college teams wouldn't swap with the females. And men sometimes are still uneasy about letting women in their games. In 2003, Annika Sorenstam, one of the world's best women golfers, jumped at a chance to play in a Professional Golf Association tournament, the Colonial, becoming the first woman since Babe Didrikson Zaharias to compete professionally against the men. Some male golfers were furious that she took a man's spot. Some observers saw another "Battle of the Sexes." But Ms. Sorenstam, who already had won forty-three women's tournaments, simply wanted to see what she could do in a tougher league.

She played well the first day but slipped on the second and failed to make the cut to go on. In two days, though, she won the hearts of fans who saw not a publicity stunt, but an athlete pushing herself to her limits. Not long after, a fourteen-year-old golfing phenomenon named Michelle Wie, playing as an amateur, became the youngest person ever to play in a men's professional golf tournament— and missed the cut by just one stroke. In playing with the best men in the world, each athlete was testing all her skills and talents.

At its heart, Title IX tries to do the same thing. Though the effort is sometimes awkward and bureaucratic, the

instant replay

An Old Friend, a New Name

On June 23, 2002, U.S. Representative Patsy Mink recognized the anniversary of Title IX by recounting its difficult history to the House of Representatives. "While the story of Title IX is a story of celebration, it is also a story of struggle to defend it against persistent challenges," she said. "For thirty years, we have constantly needed to be on guard to defend it."

From Edith Green's hearings on discrimination against women in schools through the many legislative battles and skirmishes, "the pursuit and enforcement of Title IX has been a personal crusade for me," she said. Long after Mrs. Green retired, Mrs. Mink fought for Title IX through two stints in Congress.

Mrs. Mink called on her congressional colleagues to "rededicate ourselves to the goals of dignity, equality, and opportunity for all that characterized our dreams for Title IX thirty years ago. These goals are every bit as worthy and important today, in 2002, as they were in 1972."

Three months later Mrs. Mink passed away at the age of seventy-four from pneumonia. She had served a total of twenty-four years in the House.

Her colleagues hailed her passion, her commitment, and her pioneering efforts on behalf of women, children, and working families. They also remembered her "heroic, visionary, and tireless leadership" in supporting Title IX in a very special way. In October 2002, Congress passed a law, signed by President George W. Bush, giving Title IX another name: the Patsy Takemoto Mink Equal Opportunity in Education Act.

Right: Fourteen-year-old Michelle Wie, playing as an amateur against male professionals, wows the crowd at the Sony Open in January 2004. Michelle is one of a new generation of girls poised to take women's athletics to new levels.

law seeks to boldly break down old barriers and make sure schools are places where both boys and girls can grow and excel.

As girls and women make progress, closing the last gaps in opportunities and uprooting the most entrenched attitudes gets harder, like running the last mile of a very long race. Both sexes will probably continue to struggle with how much is enough. Both will continue to redefine what boys and girls—and men and women—can do. But ultimately, the true goal of equal opportunity is a simple one: the hope that someday all boys and girls will have the chance to find out just how good they can really be.

a title ix time line

1848: About three hundred people gather in Seneca Falls, NY, in the first women's rights convention in the United States.

1869: Congress approved the Fifteenth Amendment to the Constitution, giving black men, but not black or white women, the right to vote.

1900: Women compete in the modern Olympics for the first time.

1920: States approve the Nineteenth Amendment to the Constitution, giving women the right to vote.

1923: The Equal Rights Amendment is first proposed in Congress.

1954: Edith Starrett Green is elected to Congress.

1958: Responding to an "education emergency" prompted by Russia's launch of the satellite *Sputnik,* Congress passes the National Defense Education Act to improve education in math, science, and foreign languages.

1963: Betty Friedan's book, *The Feminine Mystique*, is published.

The President's Commission on the Status of Women finds that women are discriminated against in schools and at work, and it calls for more opportunities in education and fairer pay.

Congress passes the Equal Pay Act, requiring employers to pay male and female hourly workers the same wages for the same work.

1964: Congress passes the Civil Rights Act to address racial discrimination. The act includes a provision barring employers from discriminating against women in employment.

1966: The National Organization for Women is formed.

1970: U.S. Representative Edith Green holds the first congressional hearings on women in education.

1971: The House of Representatives approves the Education Amendments, which include Title IX, banning sex discrimination in education.

1972: The Congress approves the Equal Rights Amendment, sending it to the states for approval.

The Senate approves Title IX.

President Richard Nixon signs the Education Amendments of 1972 and Title IX into law.

1973: Billie Jean King defeats Bobby Riggs in the "Battle of the Sexes."

1974: Caspar W. Weinberger, secretary of Health, Education, and Welfare, announces the proposed rules for Title IX, including the requirement that schools must offer sports for girls if they offer them for boys.

Edith Green retires from Congress.

1975: President Gerald R. Ford approves the Title IX rules.

Despite strong opposition from the National Collegiate Athletic Association, Congress declines to change or water down the Title IX rules regarding sports and PE.

1979: After much discussion, HEW Secretary Patricia Roberts Harris introduces a three-prong test to measure whether schools are complying with Title IX. Schools must meet at least one of the three tests to comply with the law.

Congress extends the deadline for states to approve the ERA.

1982: The ERA fails to win the support of thirty-eight states.

For the first time, more women earn bachelor's degrees than men.

1983: The U.S. Supreme Court agrees to hear the case of Grove City College, which is challenging Title IX's broad application.

1984: The U.S. Supreme Court rules in the Grove City case that Title IX applies only to programs that directly receive federal funds. Most sports programs don't receive federal money.

U.S. women star in the Los Angeles Olympics, calling new attention to women athletes.

1987: Edith Green dies.

1988: Congress passes the Civil Rights Restoration Act, extending Title IX to all of a school's programs, if the school receives federal money.

1992: A study finds teachers still have higher expectations for boys than girls, calling on them more often and encouraging them more.

1996: "Title IX babies" are the darlings of the Atlanta Olympics, winning gold in gymnastics, softball, basketball, soccer, and synchronized swimming.

1999: The U.S. women's soccer team fills huge stadiums on the way to winning the Women's World Cup, ushering in a new era for women in sports.

2003: After a year-long review of Title IX rules, prompted by complaints of discrimination against men's wrestling and gymnastics teams, U.S. Education Secretary Rod Paige quietly decides to leave Title IX rules alone, saying the law enjoys "very broad support."

then and now

What they said then:	**What they say now:**
Then (1973):	**Now:**
Doris Brown Heritage,	"We are second-class in some ways,
Running champion and coach	but then, probably, males are in
"Most of us feel that being second-class citizens would be a great advance. . . . Second-class citizenship sounds good when you are accustomed to being regarded as fifth-class."	some ways too. I think we are much closer to being of the same class."
Then (1973):	**Now:**
Dr. Creighton J. Hale,	Letting girls into Little League
Little League president	is "one of the best things that
"There are differences between the male and female, in spite of the trend now to try and say there aren't any differences." Boys, he said, have more muscle by age ten than girls and can run faster, hit harder, and react more quickly.	happened." One of his five granddaughters played Little League ball in Ohio, becoming the first girl ever selected to the tournament team there. "What goes around, comes around," he said.
Then (1971):	**Now:**
John N. Erlenborn,	"That sounds pretty good."
U.S. representative from Illinois	Does he still agree with that?
"I feel that if Congress permits the Federal Government to take away from colleges their right to determine the composition of their own student bodies, it will plant the seed of destruction for our system of higher education as we know it."	"To a great extent, yes."

Then (1971):

Marlyn McGrath Lewis,
Harvard University

"Since women have been much less inclined than men to concentrate in the sciences, a heavy substitution of women for men might underutilize our science faculties and require expensive additions to our faculty and staff in already crowded departments in the humanities and social sciences. . . . In the longer run, there may be an even more serious risk of substantially impairing the level of alumni support to the University."

Now:

"This describes a thinking from a world that is barely recognizable today. We run a fully coeducational college with sex-blind, equal-access admissions," says Marlyn McGrath Lewis, admissions director for Harvard College. In 2004, Harvard admitted more female undergraduates than males for the first time in its history.

Then (1984):

William Bradford "Brad" Reynolds, Civil
Rights Division, U.S. Justice Department

"I don't think it will have any impact at all," he said of the Supreme Court's Grove City ruling, which limited Title IX's reach. "I don't think you have a lot of individuals trying to think up ways to discriminate against women."

Now:

Grove City was "the right call at the right time," he says. But he also credits Title IX for giving women valuable experience in team sports and diversifying schools and professions. "My view is, in every respect, it has had a positive impact."

Then (1971):

Patsy Mink, U.S. representative
from Hawaii

"Millions of women pay taxes into the Federal treasury and we collectively resent that these funds should be used for the support of institutions to which we are denied equal access. . . . This is all that the provision of this bill requires—fairness and impartiality. . . . If we really believe in equality, we must begin to insist that our institutions of higher learning practice it or not come to the Federal Government for financial support."

Now (2002):

"While it is wonderful that equity has become the expected norm, we must also teach each new generation that there was a time when Title IX did not exist. Further, we all need to be reminded that since Title IX was put in place by a legislative body, it can also be taken away by a legislative body. We need to be vigilant. Title IX must be protected and defended to ensure that equal educational opportunities for girls and women are preserved for all generations to come."

a personal note

Edith Green, the mother of Title IX, believed that history, and especially recent history, teaches valuable lessons. She was especially fond of a particular saying: "The trouble with every generation is that they haven't read the minutes of the last meeting." With my two daughters entering their teens, I embarked on this project to share the minutes of the modern women's movement with the current generation.

Title IX was particularly significant for me because we grew up together. I first read about it in high school and first wrote about it for my college newspaper. Over three decades millions of words have since been written about this controversial law. But as the years passed the story of its history was disappearing.

I am enormously indebted to the many dedicated people who helped me report and tell this story. Bunny Sandler pointed me to academic papers and spent hours filling me in on the details of her experience. Margaret Dunkle also was generous with her time and help, recommending other sources and sharing a fabulous file of related cartoons. Melinda Grenier navigated the Schlesinger Library at Harvard to dig gems out of Ms. Dunkle's papers there.

Margot Friedman and Marcia Greenberger of the National Women's Law Center shared their extensive legislative notebooks and their copy machine. Marjorie Snyder and Yolanda Jackson at the Women's Sports Foundation gave me free rein of their clipping files and shared athletic sources. The amazing librarians in the Dallas Public Library's Interlibrary Loan office tracked down books all over Texas.

Shawna Gandy and her colleagues at the Oregon Historical Society graciously made special accommodations so I could study Edith Green's papers. Mary Mazzio of 50 Eggs and my colleagues Emily Nelson and Melinda Beck gave key assistance on the Yale crew story. Bill Sanders, Clay Bennett, and Jeff Millar helped locate elusive cartoons.

Above: A "Stone Soup" cartoon by Jan Eliot in 1999.

As the story took shape Candace Fleming, Patricia Hinton, Kathy Wendling, and Ann Zimmerman shared valuable insights and ideas. My editor, Caitlyn Dlouhy, was unwavering in her support. Most of all, I am grateful to my husband, Scott, and my daughters, Abby and Jenny, for their enthusiasm, perceptive critiques, and unconditional hugs. They are truly a blessing.

As I researched this book many people asked, "Do your daughters play sports?" After dabbling in soccer, softball, basketball, and volleyball, they each settled on their first love, ballet, as their preferred physical activity. But they had both a chance and a choice—and that makes all the difference.

Karen Blumenthal
Dallas, Texas

source notes

The material in this book was drawn from interviews, newspaper and magazine articles, oral histories and autobiographies, and a handful of academic papers and dissertations. Because memories grow fuzzy over three decades and published information can be inaccurate, I sought at least two sources on each point of fact whenever possible.

Details and quotations from congressional debates came mostly from the *Congressional Record*. That record, I learned, comes with a disclaimer. Senators and representatives may correct, add to, or even make wholesale changes in their remarks before they are printed in the *Congressional Record*. Despite efforts over many years to make this publication a word-for-word reflection of what was said, it remains only "substantially" accurate. Today, with television cameras following every act of Congress, legislators are less likely to rewrite or add to their words. But in the 1970s that practice was common, and there is no way to know what exactly was said on the floor and what wasn't. Even so, the *Congressional Record* remains the best record available.

The growth of computers in the 1980s and of the Internet in the 1990s has changed the way research can be done, making documents, articles, and other information far more accessible than ever before. I made extensive use of Factiva, a subscription database of newspaper and magazine articles dating back to the mid-1980s. This service may also be available at many public libraries. When material was accessed from the Internet, I included the links, but there are no guarantees those links will remain active indefinitely.

It would be overwhelming to list every resource consulted in pulling this story together. The citations below reflect sources of facts or quotations used in the text. In addition, more than three dozen people granted interviews, and while not all of them were quoted, all of them provided useful insight. A list of those interviewed appears at the end of these notes.

INTRODUCTION
Quote: Anna Quindlen, "Horrors! Girls with Gavels!" *Newsweek,* April 15, 2002, p. 64.
Statistics: National Federation of State High School Associations, "2002–03 Athletics Participation Summary," retrieved online from www.nfhs.org.
On Mink's warning: Patsy Mink, "In Celebration of the 30th Anniversary of Title IX of the Education Amendments of 1972," speech to the U.S. House of Representatives, *Congressional Record,* July 17, 2002, pp. H4860–H4863, accessible online at www.gpoaccess.gov/crecord/index.html.

CHAPTER 1
Quote: Eleanor Roosevelt in Margaret Mead and Frances Balgley Kaplan, *American Women: The Report of the President's Commission on the Status of Women and Other Publications of the Commission* (New York: Charles Scribner's Sons, 1965), p. 15.
On Donna de Varona: Donna de Varona, "I Hit That Turn, Gung Ho, Guts Out!" *Life,* October 9, 1964, pp. 104–105. Barbara Heilman, "Still on Top at 14," *Sports Illustrated*, April 16, 1962, pp. 26–39. Marty Benson, "Former Olympian to Be Honored as Roosevelt Recipient," *NCAA News,* December 9, 2002, retrieved online at www.ncaa.org. Frank Deford, *The Heart of a Champion: Celebrating the Spirit and Character of Great American Sports Heroes.* (San Diego, CA: Tehabi Books, 2002), pp. 82–85. Interview with Donna de Varona, July 28, 2003, and biography provided by her.

CHAPTER 2
Quote: Shirley Chisholm, "Equal Rights for Women," presented to the U.S. House of Representatives, May 21, 1969, retrieved online from Duke University's Special Collections Library at http://scriptorium.lib.duke.edu/wlm/.
On Seneca Falls and Susan B. Anthony: Eleanor Flexner, *Century of Struggle: The Woman's Rights Movement in the United States* (Cambridge, MA: Belknap Press, 1966), pp. 74–77. Sue Heinemann, *The New York Public Library Amazing Women in American History: A Book of Answers for Kids* (New York: John Wiley & Sons, 1998), pp. 34–37, 46–48, 97–99. Geoffrey C. Ward and Ken Burns, *Not for Ourselves Alone: The Story of Elizabeth Cady Stanton and Susan B.*

Anthony (New York: Alfred A. Knopf, 1999), pp. 38–42, 212.

The 1920s to 1960s: Ruth Rosen, *The World Split Open: How the Modern Women's Movement Changed America* (New York: Penguin Books, 2000), pp. 41–42. *American Women;* pp. 26–32, 86–95; this report grew out of a commission created by President John F. Kennedy to assess the status of American women and offers a clear-eyed look at where women had been and where they were in education, the workforce, and at home.

On the Civil Rights Act of 1964: Martha W. Griffiths, unpublished article on how the word "sex" was included in the Civil Rights Act, included as appendix 1 to Emily George and Fern S. Ingersoll, interviewers, Oral History Interview with Martha W. Griffiths, Member of Congress from Michigan, 1955 to 1975, conducted by Emily George from December 1977 to April 1978, and with Fern S. Ingersoll in October 1979. Sponsored by Former Members of Congress Inc. as part of its Modern Congress in American History project, pp. 5–11, 15–17. Flora Davis, *Moving the Mountain: The Women's Movement in America Since 1960* (New York: Simon & Schuster, 1991), pp. 38–45. Rosen, *The World Split Open,* pp. 70–80. John Beckler, "LBJ Signs," Associated Press newswire, July 2, 1964, retrieved online from www.epals.com/20thcentury/64rightsbill.tpl.

On Shirley Ann Jackson: Interview with Shirley Ann Jackson, July 23, 2003. Also, Susan A. Ambrose, Kristin L. Dunkle, Barbara A. Lazarus, Indira Nair, and Deborah A. Harkus, *Journeys of Women in Science and Engineering: No Universal Constants* (Philadelphia: Temple University Press, 1977), pp. 228–232.

On Susan Love: Interview with Susan Love, July 31, 2003. Also, Ambrose et al., *Journeys of Women,* pp. 262–271.

On the mid-1960s: Data from the Bureau of Labor Statistics, U.S. Department of Labor, retrieved online from www.bls.gov. Davis, *Moving the Mountain,* pp. 45–55. Heinemann, *Amazing Women,* pp. 137–139.

PLAYER PROFILE: MYRA BRADWELL

Jane M. Friedman, *America's First Woman Lawyer: The Biography of Myra Bradwell* (Buffalo, NY: Prometheus Books, 1993), pp. 17–30. Karen DeCrow, *Sexist Justice: How Legal Sexism Affects You* (New York: Vintage Books, 1975), pp. 30–35. Hedda Garza, *Barred from the Bar: A History of Women and the Legal Profession* (New York: Franklin Watts, 1996), p. 10.

PLAYER PROFILE: MARTHA WRIGHT GRIFFITHS

Emily George, *Martha W. Griffiths* (Lanham, MD: University Press of America, 1982), pp. 2–3, 143–210. Davis, *Moving the Mountain,* p. 124. Esther Stineman, *American Political Women: Contemporary and Historical Profiles* (Littleton, CO: Libraries Unlimited, 1980), p. 56.

INSTANT REPLAY: FOR MEMBERS ONLY

Fern S. Ingersoll, interviewer, Oral History Interview with Patsy T. Mink, Member of Congress from Hawaii, 1965 to 1977, conducted on March 6, March 26, and June 7, 1979, and sponsored by Former Members of Congress Inc. as part of its Modern Congress in American History project, pp. 110–112.

INSTANT REPLAY: LIBBERS AND BRA BURNERS

Charlotte Curtis, "Miss America Is Picketed by 100 Women," *New York Times,* September 8, 1969, p. 81. "Women's Liberation Group Protests Beauty Pageant," *Washington Post,* September 9, 1968, p. B2. Davis, *Moving the Mountain,* p. 107.

CHAPTER 3

Quote: Edith Green made similar statements many times during her career. This particular version comes from her "Fears and Fallacies: Equal Opportunities in the 1970s," the Ninth Annual William K. McInally Memorial Lecture, given to the University of Michigan Graduate School of Business Administration, October 31, 1974, p. 15.

On the school superintendent: Shirley Tanzer, interviewer, Oral History Interview with Edith Green, Member of Congress from Oregon, 1955 to 1975, conducted from November 18, 1978, to March 18, 1980, and sponsored by Former Members of Congress Inc. as part of its Modern Congress in American History project, pp. 101–102. Also, a similar version is in Cynthia E. Harrison, Interview with Edith Green, December 18, 1978, for the Oregon Historical Society Research Library, p. 18.

On Edith Green's background: Tanzer, Oral History Interview with Edith Green, 1978–1980, pp. 12–13, 22. Bill Keller, "Edith Green: Major Sacrifices Required to Solve World Problems," *Sunday Oregonian,* December 29, 1974, p. D1. John Painter Jr., "A Synonym for Oregon: Congresswoman Green Focused on Education," obituary in *Oregonian,* April 22, 1987, p. B8.

About her work as a legislator: John Beckler, "Rep. Edith Green Well-Liked," *Oregonian,* May 22, 1962, sec. 2, p. 1. Bill Keller, "Our Mrs. Green Will Leave Her Mark in Washington, Plus Some Sighs of Relief Among the Well-Earned Roses," *Sunday Oregonian,* May 12, 1974, from the Oregon Historical Society Research Library. Norman C. Miller, "Rep. Edith Green, a Bareknuckle Fighter," *The Wall Street Journal,* December 3, 1969, p. 18.

Quote from congressional aide: Bill Robertson, "Rep. Green Leader in Women's Rights," *Oregon Journal,* October 14, 1971, sec. 2, p. 4.

INSTANT REPLAY: THE EQUAL PAY ACT

"Congress Urged to Equalize Pay for Equal Work by Both Sexes," *New York Times,* May 27, 1955, p. 26. National Committee on Pay Equity, retrieved online at www.pay-equity.org. Edith Green speech at the White House on the effective date of the Equal Pay Legislation, June 11, 1964. Edith Green Papers, MSS 1424, Oregon Historical Society Research Library, p. 1. Tanzer, Oral History Interview with Edith Green, 1978–1980, pp. 89–92. Harrison, Interview with Green, December 18, 1978, p. 4, 15. "The 'Equal Pay' Law: How It Will Work," *U.S. News & World Report,* June 24, 1963, p. 10.

CHAPTER 4

Quote: Speech by Edith Green to the National Association of State Universities and Land-Grant Colleges, New Orleans, November 8, 1971, Edith Green Papers, MSS 1424, Oregon Historical Society Research Library, p. 10.

On Mrs. Green and Dr. Sandler: Interviews with Bernice Sandler, November 5, 2002, and February 12, 2003. Bernice R. Sandler, "'Too Strong for a Woman'—The Five Words That Created Title IX," retrieved online from www.bernicesandler.com.

The 1970 hearings: Special Subcommittee on Education of the Committee on Education and Labor, U.S. House of Representatives, *Discrimination Against Women,* 91st Congress, part I, pp. 49, 299–300, 304. Catharine R. Stimpson, *Discrimination Against Women: Congressional Hearings on Equal Rights in Education and Employment* (New York: R. R. Bowker Co., 1973), pp. xiii–xvii. Also, Interviews with Sandler, November 5, 2002, and February 12, 2003.

Statistic on doctors: "The Bars Against Women," *Time,* January 11, 1971, p. 31–32.

Legislative history: Tanzer, Oral History Interview with Edith Green, 1978–1980, pp. 101–103. Green's speech, New Orleans, November 8, 1971, p. 2. Interviews with Sandler, November 5, 2002, and February 12, 2003.

Editorials: "Sex Balance by Edict," *New York Times,* August 15, 1971, sec. 4, p. 14; and "Women's Rights and the Colleges," *Washington Post,* September 16, 1971, p. A18.

Debate in the House: *Congressional Record,* November 4, 1971, pp. 39248–39261, 39352–39354.

Harvard admissions, letter, and response: Albin Krebs, "Notes on People," *New York Times,* October 7, 1971, p. 62. *Congressional Record,* November 1, 1971, p. 38639. "Equal Admissions," *Harvard Crimson,* October 21, 1971, retrieved online from www.thecrimson.com.

Position of Yale, Princeton, Notre Dame: *Congressional Record,* November 1, 1971, p. 38640, and November 4, 1971, pp. 39248–39250.

On Stanford University: Interview with Gwendolyn Mink, December 12, 2002. *Congressional Record,* November 4, 1971, p. 39252.

Response to Erlenborn vote: Eric Wentworth, "House Adds Bus Curb to School Bill," *Washington Post,* November 5, 1971, pp. A1, A13. Bella S. Abzug, *Bella! Ms. Abzug Goes to Washington* (New York: Saturday Review Press, 1972), p. 268. *Congressional Record,* November 5, 1971, pp. 39672–39673. Tanzer, Oral History Interview with Edith Green, 1978–1980, p. 103

INSTANT REPLAY: CROSS-COUNTRY IN CONNECTICUT

E-mail correspondence with William F. Gallagher, lawyer for Susan Hollander. Brief to the Supreme Court, State of Connecticut, in *Susan Hollander v. The Connecticut Interscholastic Athletic Conference, et al.,* March 8, 1972, pp. 8–16.

PLAYER PROFILE: RUTH BADER GINSBURG

Garza, *Barred from the Bar,* p. 127. Biography at www.supremecourthistory.org. Miriam Schneir, *Feminism in Our Time: The Essential Writings, World War II to the Present* (New York: Vintage Books, 1994), pp. 481–483.

PLAYER PROFILE: PATSY TAKEMOTO MINK

Ingersoll, Oral History Interview with Patsy T. Mink, 1979, pp. 7, 52–53. Interview with G. Mink, December 12, 2002. Christina Looper Baker and Christina Baker Kline, *The Conversation Begins: Mothers and Daughters Talk About Living Feminism* (New York: Bantam Books, 1997), pp. 49–55.

CHAPTER 5

Quote: The introduction to Title IX of the Education Amendments of 1972. Available online in numerous places, including www.usdoj.gov/crt/cor/coord/titleix.htm.

Birch Bayh and the Senate: Letters between Edith Green and Birch Bayh, October 8, 1971, and September 14, 1971, from Edith Green Papers, MSS 1424, Oregon Historical Society Research Library. *Congressional Record,* August 5, 1971, p. 30155, and August 6, 1971, pp. 30403–30415. Interview with Birch Bayh, November 4, 2002.

High school statistics: National Federation of State High School Associations, "1971 Sports Participation Survey."

Swimming World **magazine:** From Edith Green Papers, MSS 1424, Oregon Historical Society Research Library.

Dominick's questions: *Congressional Record,* August 6, 1971, pp. 30406–30408.

Bayh's additional efforts: *Congressional Record,* November 24, 1971, pp. 43080–43081, and February 28, 1972, pp. 5803–58015.

On Green's efforts: Keller, "Our Mrs. Green," Tanzer, Oral History Interview with Edith Green, 1978–1980, pp. 103–106.

Final vote in the House: *Congressional Record,* June 8, 1972, pp. 20282–20340. Eric Wentworth, "Aid to Education, Busing Curb Pass," *Washington Post,* June 9, 1972, pp. A1, A8. Phil Cogswell, "Edith Green Leads Futile Last-Minute Effort to Kill Bill She Helped Draft," *Oregonian,* June 9, 1972, p. 6. David E. Rosenbaum, "House Votes Bill to Block Busing; Sends It to Nixon," *New York Times,* June 9, 1972, pp. 1, 16.

Nixon signs: Eric Wentworth, "Nixon Signs Busing Bill Reluctantly," *Washington Post,* June 24, 1972, pp. A1, A4. Eric Wentworh, "New Programs to Make Mark on Education," *Washington Post,* June 24, 1972, p. A4. Robert B. Semple Jr., "President Signs School Aid Bill; Scores Congress," *New York Times,* June 24, 1972, pp. 1, 15.

PLAYER PROFILE: BIRCH BAYH

Interview with Bayh, November 4, 2002.

INSTANT REPLAY: DON'T CALL ME BOB

Interview with Richardson, November 1, 2002; Dot Richardson, with Don Yaeger, *Living the Dream* (New York: Kensington Books, 1997), pp. 19–22.

INSTANT REPLAY: THE FIGHT FOR EQUAL RIGHTS
George and Ingersoll, Oral History Interview with Martha W. Griffiths, pp. 80–84. George, *Martha W. Griffiths,* pp. 167–172. Davis, *Moving the Mountain,* pp. 123–128.

INSTANT REPLAY: TITLE IX
Myra E. Barrer, ed., *Journal of Reprints of Documents Affecting Women,* vol. 1, no.1 (July 1976): 267–271.

CHAPTER 6
Quote: Sally Jenkins, "Title IX Opponents a Bunch of Sad Sacks," *Washington Post,* June 24, 2002, p. D1, retrieved online via Factiva and confirmed in interview with Billie Jean King.
HEW process: Interview with Caspar W. Weinberger, January 7, 2003. Andrew Fischel and Janice Pottker, "Sex Discrimination and the Administrative Rule-Making Process: The Development of the Title IX Regulation," in *National Politics and Sex Discrimination in Education* (Lexington, MA: Lexington Books, 1977), pp. 105–113. Margaret Dunkle and Jill Reid, Interview with Martin Gerry, Former Deputy Director of HEW's Office for Civil Rights, August 19, 1985. Margaret Dunkle Papers (unpublished), Schlesinger Library, Radcliffe Institute, Harvard University.
On basketball: Joanne Lannin, *A History of Basketball for Girls and Women: From Bloomers to Big Leagues* (Minneapolis, MN: LernerSports, 2000), p. 28.
On sports in the early part of the century: Lannin, *History of Basketball,* p. 12. Susan K. Cahn, *Coming on Strong: Gender and Sexuality in Twentieth-Century Women's Sport* (New York: Free Press, 1994), pp. 55–65. Mary L. Motley and Mary E. Lavine, "Century Marathon: A Race for Equality in Girls' and Women's Sports," *Journal of Physical Education, Recreation & Dance* (August 1, 2001): 56–59, retrieved online via Factiva.
Babe Didrikson: Russell Freedman, *Babe Didrikson Zaharias: The Making of a Champion* (New York: Clarion Books, 1999), pp. 84–85. Dave Anderson, *The Story of the Olympics* (New York: HarperCollinsPublishers, 2000).
On Tara VanDerveer: Tara VanDerveer, with Joan Ryan, *Shooting from the Outside: How a Coach and Her Olympic Team Transformed Women's Basketball* (New York: Avon Books, 1997), pp. 35–38.
Christine Grant: Interview with Christine H. B. Grant, December 11, 2002.
Billie Jean King: Interview with Billie Jean King, January 28, 2003. Billie Jean King, with Kim Chapin, *Billie Jean* (New York: Harper & Row Publishers, 1974), pp. 140–186. Billie Jean King, "My Favorite Chauvinist," *Sports Illustrated,* November 6, 1995, p. 118. Curry Kirkpatrick, "There She Is, Ms. America," *Sports Illustrated,* October 1, 1973, retrieved online from www.CNNSI.com.
HEW: See sources for HEW process above in chapter 6's notes. Caspar W. Weinberger, with Gretchen Roberts, *In the Arena: A Memoir of the 20th Century* (Washington, DC: Regnery Publishing, 2001), pp. 223–224.

PLAYER PROFILE: DORIS BROWN HERITAGE
Interview with Heritage, November 29, 2002. Bil Gilbert and Nancy Williamson, "Sport Is Unfair to Women," *Sports Illustrated,* May 28, 1973, p. 90.

INSTANT REPLAY: WOMEN IN THE OLYMPICS
Jane Leder, *Grace & Glory: A Century of Women in the Olympics* (Chicago: Triumph Books, 1996), pp. 6, 10–11. Allen Guttman, *Women's Sports: A History* (New York: Columbia University Press, 1991), p. 169. The Olympic Web site at www.olympic.org offers brief histories of many individual sports.

INSTANT REPLAY: LITTLE LEAGUE
"Alumni Profile: Maria Pepe," *FDU, (Fairleigh Dickinson University) Magazine* (Fall/Winter 1998), retrieved online at www.fdu.edu. Joseph B. Treaster, "Women Make Strides: On Bases and into Mory's," *New York Times,* March 30, 1974, pp. 1, 25. Robert W. Peterson, "'You Really Hit That One, Man!' Said the Little League Boy to the Little League Girl," *New York Times Magazine,* May 19, 1974, pp. 36–37, 90. Joseph B. Treaster, "Little League Baseball Yields to 'Social Climate' and Accepts Girls," *New York Times,* June 11, 1974, p. 26. Lance Van Auken and Robin Van Auken, *Play Ball! The Story of Little League Baseball* (University Park: Pennsylvania State University Press, 2001), pp. 145–154.

PLAYER PROFILE: BILLIE JEAN KING
Interview with King, January 28, 2003. Paul Reinhard, "Billie Jean Still in Search of Equality," *Allentown Morning Call,* October 25, 2002, p. C2, retrieved online via Factiva.

CHAPTER 7
Quote: In Ellen Weber, "The Title IX Controversy," *WomenSports* (June 1974): 74–77.
On the NCAA: "HEW Regulations Threaten College Athletics," *NCAA News,* pp. 2–3, retrieved online from www.ncaa.org. Weber, "Title IX Controversy." Associated Press, "'Equal' Rules for Women Create College Problem," *New York Times,* May 12, 1974, clipping, and NCAA memorandum to chief executive officers of NCAA member institutions, February 21, 1974, both from the Women's Sports Foundation files.
Statistics on sports: Gilbert and Williamson, "Sport Is Unfair to Women," pp. 88–98. Nancy Scannell and Bart Barnes, "The Girls in the Locker Room: The Financial Bind," *Washington Post,* May 14, 1974, pp. A1, A10. "Locker Room Lib," *Time,* March 11, 1974, p. 73.
The Tower amendment: Fischel and Pottker, "Sex Discrimination," pp. 109–114. *Congressional Record,* May 20, 1974, pp. 15322–15323. Nancy Scannell, "Senate Passes Title 9 Proviso," *Washington Post,* May 21, 1974, clipping from the Women's Sports Foundation files. Interview with Margot Polivy, December 3, 2002.

On HEW's proposed rules: Eileen Shanahan, "H.E.W. Proposes Rules to Outlaw Schools' Sex Bias," *New York Times*, June 19, 1974, pp. 1, 32. Eric Wentworth, "U.S. Sets Curbs on Sex Bias," *Washington Post,* June 19, 1974, pp. A1, A22. "Statements by Caspar W. Weinberger, Secretary, Department of Health, Education and Welfare, at a Press Briefing, June 18, 1974," Women's Sports Foundation files.

After the rules proposed: Interview with Weinberger, January 7, 2003. Interviews with Sandler, November 5, 2002, and February 12, 2003. Fischel and Pottker, "Sex Discrimination," pp. 114–116.

On Princeton admissions: United Press International; "Women Enrollment in Law Schools Up," *Washington Post,* January 12, 1974, p. A3. Associated Press, "Princeton to Lift Quota on Women," *Washington Post,* January 21, 1974, p. A16.

Final regulations: Gerald Eskanazi, "Title IX Rules Issued for Equality in Sports," *New York Times,* June 4, 1975, pp. 29, 30. Nancy Scannell and Eric Wentworth, two stories under the headline "New HEW Rules Bar Sex Bias in Nation's Schools," *Washington Post,* June 4, 1975, pp. A1, A9, A11.

Final battles before the regulations became effective: Interviews with Sandler, November 5, 2002, and February 12, 2003. Interview with Margaret Dunkle, January 17, 2003. Mary Ann Millsap, "Sex Equity in Education," in *Women in Washington: Advocates for Public Policy,* ed. Irene Tinker (Beverly Hills, CA: Sage Publications, 1983), pp. 97–101. Also, Mary Ann Millsap, "Advocates for Sex Equity in Federal Education Law: The National Coalition for Women and Girls in Education," Ed.D. diss., Harvard University, 1988, pp. 31–48. Associated Press, "Hearings Commence Today on New Title 9 Regulations; Texas' Royal to Testify," *Washington Post,* June 17, 1975, p. D7. House Committee on Education and Labor, statement of Darrell Royal, President, American Football Coaches Association, in *Sex Discrimination Regulations: Hearings Before the Subcommittee on Postsecondary Education,* June 17, 1975, pp. 46–50. Eric Wentworth, "Bill Would Limit Sex Bias Law's Impact on Colleges," *Washington Post,* July 8, 1975, p. D4. Nancy Scannell, "House Panel Stymies Effort to Weaken School Sex-Bias Rules," *Washington Post*, July 10, 1975, p. A7. "Congressional Report: House Restricts HEW Rules," *Washington Post,* July 17, 975, p. A3. Nancy Hicks, "House Weakens Sex-Bias Rules," *New York Times,* July 17, 1975, p. 30. *Congressional Record,* July 16, 1975, pp. 23121–23127, and July 18, 1975, pp. 23504–23510. United Press International, "All-Male Senate Rebuffs House on Sex-Segregation School Plan," *New York Times,* July 18, 1975, p. 34. Nancy Hicks, "House Reverses Itself to Allow Integration of Sexes in Schools," *New York Times,* July 19, 1975, p. 26. Eric Wentworth, "Ban on Sex Integration Is Rejected," *Washington Post,* July 19, 1975, pp. A1, A3.

INSTANT REPLAY: LOOKING FOR A LITTLE RESPECT
Suzanne Levine and Harriet Lyons, ed., *The Decade of Women: A* Ms. *History of the Seventies in Words and Pictures* (New York: G. P. Putnam's Sons, 1980), p. 71. Reprinted by permission of *Ms.* magazine, 1973.

INSTANT REPLAY: SAVING THE SCOUTS
Congressional Record, November 18, 1974, p. 36167; November 26, 1974, pp. 37384–37386; December 16, 1974, pp. 39991–39994; and December 19, 1974, pp. 41389–41394. Edward B. Fiske, "Congress Moves to Modify Law Restricting Sex Bias by Schools," *New York Times,* November 25, 1974, p. 23.

INSTANT REPLAY: FEMALE CADETS
James Feron, "Fashion, if Not Tradition, Ready for Women Cadets at West Point," *New York Times,* November 21, 1975, p. 45. "As All the Service Academies Go Co-Ed—," *U.S. News & World Report,* February 16, 1976, pp. 67–68. "Beauties and the Beast," *Time,* July 19, 1976, p. 74.

CHAPTER 8
Quote: In "Comes the Revolution," *Time,* June 26, 1978, p. 54.
Yale women: *A Hero for Daisy,* video produced by 50 Eggs, available at www.aherofordaisy.com. "Oarswomen Bare All, Want March Showers," *Yale Daily News,* March 4, 1976, pp. 10, 16. Jan Hemming, "Yale Girls Strip for Showers," *New Haven Register,* March 4, 1976, pp. 1, 2. "Yale Women Strip to Protest a Lack of Crew's Showers," *New York Times,* March 4, 1976, p. 33. "Yale Women Crew to Get Locker Room," *New York Times,* March 11, 1976, p. 41. Brief telephone discussion with photographer Nina Haight Frost.
Statistics: National Center for Education Statistics, U.S. Department of Education, "Total Fall Enrollment in Degree-Granting Institutions, by Attendance Status, Sex of Student, and Control of Institution: 1947–2000," table retrieved online from www.nces.ed.gov. American Bar Association, "First Year Enrollment in ABA Approved Law Schools, 1947–2001," table retrieved online from www.abanet.org/legaled/statistics/femstats.html. Association of American Medical Colleges, "Women Applicants, Accepted Students, and Matriculants to U.S. Medical Schools."
On math: Sheila Tobias, *Overcoming Math Anxiety* (New York: W. W. Norton & Co. 1978), pp. 13, 84–88.
Sport statistics and examples: National Federation of State High School Associations, sports participation surveys (see www.nfhs.org). "Comes the Revolution," pp. 54–59. Candace Lyle Hogan, "Title IX Progress Report: Fair Shake or Shakedown?" *WomenSports* (September 1976): 50–51. "A Sporting Chance: Women's Athletics at the University of Michigan," Bentley Historical Library, University of Michigan, retrieved online at www.umich.edu. E-mail from the Bentley Historical Library reference staff, University of Michigan, February 6, 2004. Jerry Kirshenbaum, "Scorecard," *Sports Illustrated,* February 19, 1979, from the Women's Sports Foundation files. Interview with Donna Lopiano, November 8, 2002. "Stalled at the Start: Government Action on Sex Bias in the Schools," Project on Equal Education Rights, NOW Legal

Defense and Education Fund, 1978, p. 14. Marguerite Beck-Rex, "Fired Employees Win Against Schools," *In the Running,* vol. 1, no. 4 (Winter 1978): 1, 3, from the Women's Sports Foundation files. Interview with Missy Parks, June 9, 2004. Interview with Cheryl Miller, May 24, 2003.

HEW and single-sex events: Bart Barnes reporting in *Washington Post,* "Single-Sex School Event Ruled Biased," July 7, 1976, pp. A1, A5; "Ford Acts to Permit Schools to Hold Father-Son Events," July 8, 1976, pp. A1, A7; "All-Boy Choir Approved," April 14, 1977, p. A1. "A Bravo for Boys' Choirs," *Washington Post,* April 18, 1977, p. A18. *Congressional Record,* August 26, 1976, p. 27983–27988.

HEW and Mr. Califano: "Stalled at the Start," p. 8. Joseph A. Califano Jr., *Governing America: An Insider's Report from the White House and the Cabinet* (New York: Simon & Schuster, 1981), pp. 223–225, 263–268. "Duke President Seeks Support for Title IX Counterproposal," *NCAA News,* July 25, 1979, pp. 1, 3, retrieved online via www.ncaa.org/news. Associated Press, "Alternate Plan Is Offered to Comply with Title IX," *New York Times,* May 25, 1979, p. A22. Interview with Polivy, December 3, 2002.

HEW after Mr. Califano: Nancy Scannell, "Carter Meets with Women on Title 9," *Washington Post,* September 14, 1979, from the Women's Sports Foundation files. Associated Press, "Shift Seen on Title IX Fund Rules," *New York Times,* December 4, 1979, p. C15. Gordon S. White Jr., "Mrs. Harris Strengthens Title IX Policies," *New York Times,* December 5, 1979, p. B11. Millsap, "Advocates for Sex Equity," pp. 117–122.

INSTANT REPLAY: THE WARSAW TIGERS

Philip Hoose, *We Were There, Too!: Young People in U.S. History* (New York: Farrar Straus Giroux, 2001), pp. 239–243. Hoose, *Hoosiers: The Fabulous Basketball Life Of Indiana* (New York: Vintage Books, 1986), pp. 192–210. Pat McKee, "Change was slow, despite passage of landmark law," *Indianapolis News-Indianapolis Star,* June 23, 2002, p. A13. Retrieved online via Factavia.

PLAYER PROFILE: DONNA DE VARONA

Interview with de Varona, July 28, 2003, and biography provided by her. Mark McDonald, "Panel Forms Linchpin of Olympics Machine," *Dallas Morning News,* August 25, 1988, p. 1A, retrieved online via Factiva.

INSTANT REPLAY: THE ERA FAILS

Davis, *Moving the Mountain,* pp. 386–411. For background information, see www.equalrightsamendment.org/era.html.

INSTANT REPLAY: EDITH GREEN

Edith Green, "Fears and Fallacies," p. 11. Edith Green, "The Road Is Paved with Good Intentions: Title IX and What It Is Not," speech delivered at Brigham Young University, Salt Lake City, Utah, January 25, 1977, reprinted in *Vital Speeches of the Day,* March 1, 1977, pp. 302–303. Harrison, Interview with Green, December 18, 1978, p. 16

CHAPTER 9

Quote: In Ellen Goodman, "A Gold-Medal Bill," *Washington Post,* September 15, 1984, retrieved online via Factiva.

The Reagan administration: "Address Before a Joint Session of the Congress on the Program for Economic Recovery," February 18, 1981, retrieved online via www.reagan.utexas.edu/resource/speeches. Associated Press, "Reagan May Drop Title IX Athletic Rules," *San Francisco Examiner,* August 12, 1981, from the Women's Sports Foundation's files.

On Grove City College: Associated Press, "Califano Prods Schools on Sex Bias," *Washington Post,* December 2, 1977, p. A4. Associated Press, "22 Educational Facilities Face Loss of HEW Funds," *Washington Post,* December 10, 1977, p. A7. Lee Edwards, *Freedom's College: The History of Grove City College* (Washington, DC: Regnery Publishing, 2000), pp. 195–236. "Sundae Punch: Grove City vs. Form 639A," *Time,* March 24, 1980, p. 70.

Statistics: American Bar Association, www.abanet.org; Association of American Medical Colleges; Association of American Veterinary Medical Colleges; and National Federation of State High School Associations. *Congressional Record,* April 12, 1984, p. 4601.

On Dot Richardson: Interview with Richardson, November 1, 2002.

Grove City and the U.S. Supreme Court: Interview with Brad Reynolds, July 3, 2003. Charles R. Babcock, "U.S. Won't Press Sex-Bias Case," *Washington Post,* September 9, 1982, p. A23. Mary Thornton, "A Civil Rights Battle Surfaces," *Washington Post,* October 11, 1982, p. A17. Terrel H. Bell, *The Thirteenth Man: A Reagan Cabinet Memoir* (New York: Free Press, 1988), pp. 102–113. Linda Greenhouse, "High Court Backs Reagan's Position on a Sex Bias Law," *New York Times,* February 29, 1984, pp. A1, A14. Fred Barbash, "Court Restricts Application of Sex-Bias Law," *Washington Post,* February 29, 1984, retrieved online via Factiva. Robert Pear, "U.S. Rights Panel Criticizes Administration's View of Sex Bias Rule," *New York Times,* August 10, 1983, p. A16.

Fallout from Grove City: Mary Thornton, "Impact Seen on Other Minorities, Rights Lawyers Hit Sex-Bias Ruling," *Washington Post,* March 1, 1984, retrieved online via Factiva. Bob Sherwin, "What Became of Title IX? '84 Court Ruling Took the Teeth Out of Law," *Seattle Times,* June 8, 1986, retrieved online via Factiva.

On Olympic women: All retrieved online via Factiva: Goodman, "A Gold-Medal Bill." United Press International, "Demonstration Staged on Capitol Hill," *Globe and Mail,* September 12, 1984. Tony Kornheiser, "A Marathon Finish: Stars, Stripes—and Curtain Calls," *Washington Post,* August 13, 1984. Associated Press, "U.S. Athletes Taking Home 83 Gold Medals," *Omaha World-Herald,* August 13, 1984.

On response after the Grove City decision: Senator Ted Stevens in the *Congressional Record,* April 12, 1984, p. 4601. Retrieved online via Factiva. Judy Mann, "Restoring

Rights Protection," *Washington Post,* March 26, 1987, p. B3. Ruth Marcus, "Grove City Decision Has Stifled Hundreds of Bias Complaints," *Washington Post,* March 7, 1988, p. A8.

On Elizabeth Balsley: Mike DiGiovanna, "Mixing of the Sexes Often Causes Mix-Up of Minds," *Los Angeles Times,* January 8, 1986, p. 10. Bradshaw Hovey, "Girl, 15, Getting Tryout for Football Team," *Bergen (NJ) Record,* August 21, 1985, p. A1. Both retrieved online via Factiva.

On Erin Whitten: Steve Campbell, "Goal Oriented: Erin Whitten Confronts Her Olympic Challenge," *(Albany) Times Union,* December 16, 1997, p. C1, retrieved online via Factiva. Mary Turco, *Crashing the Net: The U.S. Women's Olympic Ice Hockey Team and the Road to Gold* (New York: HarperCollinsPublishers, 1999), p. 65. Craig Merz, "For This Goaltender, Gender Can Be Double-Edged Sword," *Columbus Dispatch,* November 17, 1993, p. H1, retrieved online via Factiva. Interview with Erin Whitten, July 22, 2003.

Civil Rights Restoration Act: Ruth Marcus and Helen Dewar, "Reagan Vetoes Civil Rights Restoration Act; Bill Would 'Unjustifiably Expand' Federal Power," *Washington Post,* March 17, 1988, p. A1. Helen Dewar, "Congress Overrides Civil Rights Law Veto," *Washington Post,* March 23, 1988, p. A1. Both retrieved online via Factiva.

PLAYER PROFILE: DADS
Interview with King, January 28, 2003. Interview with Fernandez, February 17, 2003.

INSTANT REPLAY: A NATIONAL SOCCER TEAM
Jere Longman, *The Girls of Summer: The U.S. Women's Soccer Team and How It Changed the World* (New York: Perennial, 2001), pp. 63–64. Grahame L. Jones, "Women's Little Trip to Italy Was Start of Something Big," *Los Angeles Times,* July 10, 1999, p. D9, retrieved online via Factiva.

PLAYER PROFILE: SALLY RIDE
Interview with Ride, August 4, 2003.

PLAYER PROFILE: EDITH GREEN
Ellen Emry Heltzel, "Ever Green: At 75, Edith Green Remains a Shrewd, Sensible Observer of Politics and Society," *Oregonian,* January 8, 1986, p. C1, from the Oregon Historical Society Research Library. Naomi Veronica Ross, "Congresswoman Edith Green on Federal Aid to Schools and Colleges: A Thesis in Higher Education," Ed.D. diss., Pennsylvania State University, May 1980, p. 3. Ken Wheeler, "Green Won't Hedge Title IX Goals," *Oregon Journal,* April 22, 1981, pp. 35, 38. Interview with Richard Green, May 26, 2003. Eleanor Boxx, "Women of Accomplishment: Education, Poverty Legislation Pushed," *Oregon Journal,* February 24, 1972, sec. 2, pp. 1, 3, from the Oregon Historical Society Research Library.

CHAPTER 10
Quote: Interview with Grant, December 11, 2002.
On the Oklahoma women's basketball team: Mike Sherman, "OU Players Sought Coaching Change," *Daily Oklahoman,* March 30, 1990. "OU Group Decries Women's Basketball Axing," *Tulsa Tribune,* March 30, 1990, p. A1. Associated Press, "OU Basketball Move Called Sexist," *Tulsa Tribune,* April 4, 1990, p. A3. "OU Women's Basketball Program Is Reinstated," *Tulsa Tribune,* April 5, 1990, p. A1, retrieved online via Factiva.
On the AAUW report: Barbara Kantrowitz, "Sexism in the Schoolhouse," *Newsweek,* February 24, 1992, p. 62. Susan Chira, "Bias Against Girls Is Found Rife in Schools, with Lasting Damage," *New York Times,* February 12, 1992, p. A1.
High school and the NCAA: Joanne M. Schrof, "A Sporting Chance?" *U.S. News & World Report,* April 11, 1994, pp. 51–53. Douglas Lederman, "'A Moral Issue,' NCAA Director Says: NCAA Releases Report on Sex Equity," *Chronicle of Higher Education,* March 18, 1992, retrieved online from the archives at www.chronicle.com.
The Brown University lawsuit: Ruling of the 1st Circuit U.S. Court of Appeals in *Amy Cohen, et al.,* v. *Brown University, et al.,* November 21, 1996, retrieved online from www.law.emory.edu. Maureen E. Mahoney, "The Numbers Don't Add Up: So Says a Lawyer for Brown, Which Is Fighting to Ensure Title IX Benefits for All Students," *Sports Illustrated,* May 5, 1997, p. 78. ESPN, "On Equal Ground," a special on the Brown case, broadcast June 22, 2002, video provided by the Women's Sports Foundation. Interview with Lynnette Labinger, lawyer for the Brown women athletes, February 21, 2003. Interview with Amy Cohen, February 25, 2003.
The 1996 Olympics: Jere Longman, "How the Women Won," *New York Times Magazine,* July 23, 1996, pp. 23–27. Peter King, "Ms. Popularity Victorious: U.S. Women's Teams Made Friends and Influenced People," *Sports Illustrated,* August 4, 1996, pp. 34ff., retrieved online via Factiva. VanDerveer, *Shooting from the Outside,* pp. 13–28, 260. Richardson, *Living the Dream,* pp. 99–105, 113, 139–145. Bruce Adams, "NBC Blows Softball, Plans Soccer 'Look-Ins,'" *San Francisco Examiner,* August 1, 1996, p. C3, retrieved online via Factiva. Steve Rushin, "Playing with Heart," *Sports Illustrated,* July 29, 1996, pp. 55–57. Richard Zoglin, "The Girls of Summer," *Time,* August 12, 1996, pp. 49–50. Interview with Grant, December 11, 2002.
The 1998 hockey team: Turco, *Crashing the Net,* pp. xxii–xxiii. Johnette Howard, "Golden Girls," *Sports Illustrated,* March 2, 1998, pp. 46–47.
World Cup: Interview with Mia Hamm, July 29, 2003. Bill Saporito, "Flat-Out Fantastic," *Time,* July 19, 1999, pp. 58–67. Mark Starr and Martha Brant, "It Went Down to the Wire," *Newsweek,* July 19, 1999, pp. 46–55.
On Donna de Varona: Deford, *Heart of a Champion,* p. 85. Patrick Rogers and Sue Miller, "Making Waves," *People,* May 15, 2000, p. 89, retrieved online via Factiva.

End of 1999: Michael Bamberger, "Sportswomen of the Year: Dream Come True," *Sports Illustrated,* December 20, 1999, pp. 46–52, 57–60.

PLAYER PROFILE: AMY COHEN
Interview with Cohen, February 25, 2003. Erik Brady, "Putting a Face on Title IX Lawsuit," *USA Today,* June 20, 1997, p. C1, retrieved online via Factiva.

PLAYER PROFILE: MIA HAMM
Interview with Hamm, July 29, 2003.

INSTANT REPLAY: A NEW MEANING FOR TITLE IX
Interview with Aurelia Davis, February 21, 2003. Interview with Verna Williams, lawyer for the Davis family, February 20, 2003. "Decision of the U.S. Supreme Court in *Aurelia Davis, as Next Friend of LaShonda D.,* v. *Monroe County Board of Education, et al.,*" written by Justice O'Connor, and dissenting opinion by Justice Kennedy, May 24, 1999, retrieved online via http://supct.law.cornell.edu/supct/index.html.

INSTANT REPLAY: "IF YOU LET ME PLAY"
Memo on the history of the commercial, written by a member of the Nike marketing group, provided by Nike Inc. corporate communications. The One Club for Art and Copy, *The One Show: Advertising's Best Print, Radio, and TV,* vol. 18, no. 113

EPILOGUE

Quote: Hal Bock, "Capriati: What's Title IX?" Associated Press newswire, August 30, 2002.
On Duke and University of Connecticut: Jere Longman, "No. 1 Duke Is No. 59 in UConn's Streak," *New York Times,* February 2, 2003, sec. 8, pp. 1, 2. Jere Longman, "What Women's Sports Can Be," *New York Times,* February 3, 2003, pp. D1, D5.
Academic statistics: American Bar Association, www.abanet.org; Association of American Medical Colleges, www.aamc.org; Association of American Veterinary Medical Colleges, www.aavmc.org; and National Center for Education Statistics, U.S. Department of Education, "Earned Degrees Conferred by Degree-Granting Institutions, by Level of Degree and Sex of Student: 1869–70 to 2011–12," table retrieved online from www.nces.ed.gov.
Sports statistics: See National Federation of State High School Associations and NCAA Web sites, at www.nfhs.org and www.ncaa.org, respectively.
On coaches: R. Vivian Acosta and Linda Jean Carpenter, "Women in Intercollegiate Sport: A Longitudinal Study—Twenty Five Year Update, 1977–2002," retrieved online via www.womenssportsfoundation.org.
On science education: Interview with Jackson, July 23, 2003. Interview with U.S. Senator Ron Wyden, June 16, 2003.

High school and middle school examples: Aaron Kuriloff, "Louisiana Is Slow to Foster Equality," *(New Orleans) Times-Picayune,* July 3, 2001, retrieved online via Factiva. Opinion of the U.S. District Court, Western District of Michigan, Southern Division, in *Communities for Equity v. Michigan High School Athletic Association,* December 17, 2001, retrieved online from www.michbar.org.
Backlash and controversy: Interview with Heritage, November 29, 2002. Michael Dobie, "SJU's Decision Not Clear-Cut," *Newsday,* December 15, 2002, p. B15, and Bill Finley, with Brandon Lilly, "St. John's Cites Fairness in Cutting 5 Men's Teams," *New York Times,* December 14, 2002, p. 5, both retrieved online via Factiva. *The National Wrestling Coaches Association, et al.,* v. *U.S. Department of Education,* December 16, 2002; the lawsuit was originally retrieved online at www.nwcaonline.com, but the case was dismissed by a federal court. Interview with Mike Moyer, February 27, 2003.
The Department of Education commission: Information about the commission and the commission's letter was retrieved from www.ed.gov/about/bdscomm/list/athletics /index.html. Also, Erik Brady, "Opposing Factions Trade Barbs over Final Recommendations," *USA Today,* February 27, 2003, retrieved online via www.usatoday.com. Diana Jean Schemo, "With Men in Mind, Panel Recommends Changes to Title IX," *New York Times,* February 27, 2003, p. C13. Diana Jean Schemo, "Title IX Dissenters to Issue Report Criticizing Proposed Changes to Women's Athletics," *New York Times,* February 25, 2003, p. C16.
What happens next: Interview with Donna Shalala, February 27, 2003. Interview with Norma Cantú, February 20, 2003. Michael Bamberger, "Her Best Shot," *Sports Illustrated,* June 2, 2003, p. 54. Doug Ferguson, "Wie Comes Up One Shot Short at Sony Open," Associated Press newswires, January 17, 2004.

PLAYER PROFILE: LISA LESLIE
Interview with Leslie, May 20, 2003. Biography at www.galegroup.com, under Free Resources/Women's History Month/Biographies.

PLAYER PROFILE: RON WYDEN
Interview with Wyden, June 16, 2003.

INSTANT REPLAY: AN OLD FRIEND, A NEW NAME
Mink, "In Celebration of the 30th Anniversary of Title IX." *Congressional Record,* October 7, 2002, pp. H7146–H7148. Both accessible online at www.gpoaccess.gov/crecord/index.html.

THEN AND NOW
Doris Brown Heritage: Gilbert and Williamson, "Sport Is Unfair to Women," p. 90. Interview with Heritage, November 29, 2002.
Dr. Creighton J. Hale: Van Auken and Van Auken, *Play Ball!* p. 148.
John N. Erlenborn: *Congressional Record,* November 4, 1971, p. 39249. Interview with John N. Erlenborn, February 13, 2003.

Harvard University: *Congressional Record,* November 1, 1971, p. 38639. Interview with Marlyn McGrath Lewis, May 30, 2003.

William Bradford Reynolds: Fred Barbash, "Civil Rights Chief May Favor Stiffer Ban on Sex Bias," *Washington Post,* March 2, 1984, retrieved online via Factiva. Interview with Reynolds, July 3, 2003.

Patsy Mink: *Congressional Record,* November 4, 1971, p. 39252. Mink, "In Celebration of the 30th Anniversary of Title IX," *Congressional Record,* p. H4862.

SOURCES FOR SCORECARDS

High school sport statistics: National Federation of State High School Associations, "Sports Participation Survey" and "Athletics Participation Summary" for various years. The most recent surveys are available online at www.nfhs.org.

College sports statistics: National Collegiate Athletic Association, "NCAA Sports Sponsorship and Participation Rates Report" for various years. The most recent report is online at www.ncaa.org.

Bachelor's degrees: "Earned degrees conferred by degree-granting institutions, by level of degree and sex of student: 1869–70 to 2011–12," table retrieved online from the National Center for Education Statistics, U.S. Department of Education, www.nces.ed.gov.

Law students: American Bar Association, "First Year Enrollment in ABA Approved Law Schools, 1947–2001," retrieved online from www.abanet.org/legaled/statistics.html.

Medical students: Association of American Medical Colleges, "Women Applicants, Accepted Students, and Matriculants to U.S. Medical Schools."

Veterinary students: Association of American Veterinary Medical Colleges, "Enrollment Figures on Gender."

Scorecard on 1996–97: United States General Accounting Office, "Gender Equity: Mens' and Women's Participation in Higher Education," Report to the Ranking Minority Member, Subcommittee on Criminal Justice, Drug Policy and Human Resources, Committee on Government Reform, House of Representatives, December 2000, p. 37. Retrieved online at www.gao.gov.

THE FOLLOWING PEOPLE, LISTED IN ALPHABETICAL ORDER, GENEROUSLY GRANTED INTERVIEWS:

Birch Bayh, former U.S. senator and Title IX sponsor in the Senate

Cynthia G. Brown, former deputy director, Office for Civil Rights, U.S. Department of Health, Education, and Welfare

Norma Cantú, former assistant secretary, U.S. Department of Education

Amy Cohen, former Brown University gymnast

Aurelia Davis, mother of LaShonda Davis

Donna de Varona, Olympic swimmer and longtime Title IX activist

Margaret Dunkle, early Title IX activist

John N. Erlenborn, former U.S. representative

Jamie Fasteau, senior lobbyist, AAUN, and chairwoman, National Coalition for Women and Girls in Education

Lisa Fernandez, Olympic softball star

Christine H. B. Grant, former women's athletic director, University of Iowa

Richard Green, son of Edith Green

Marcia Greenberger, co-president, National Women's Law Center

Mia Hamm, soccer superstar

Doris Brown Heritage, world-class runner and coach at Seattle Pacific University

Nancy Hogshead-Makar, Olympic swimmer and Title IX lawyer

Shirley Ann Jackson, president, Rensselaer Polytechnic Institute, and former chairwoman, U.S. Nuclear Regulatory Commission

C. Todd Jones, deputy assistant secretary for enforcement, Office for Civil Rights, U.S. Department of Education

Billie Jean King, tennis legend and founder of the Women's Sports Foundation

Lynette Labinger, lawyer representing gymnasts against Brown University

Lisa Leslie, WNBA star

Marlyn McGrath Lewis, director of admissions, Harvard College

Donna Lopiano, executive director, Women's Sports Foundation

Susan Love, breast cancer authority

Cheryl Miller, former UCLA basketball standout and television broadcaster

Gwendolyn Mink, women's studies professor and daughter of Patsy Mink

Mike Moyer, executive director, National Wrestling Coaches Association

Missy Parks, founder Title 9 Sports

Margot Polivy, former attorney for the AIAW

Brad Reynolds, former chief of the Civil Rights Division, U.S. Department of Justice

Dot Richardson, Olympic softball standout and orthopedic surgeon

Sally Ride, former astronaut

Bernice Sandler, early Title IX activist and former aide to Edith Green

Donna Shalala, president, University of Miami, and former secretary, Department of Health and Human Services

Caspar W. Weinberger, former secretary, U.S. Department of Health, Education, and Welfare

Erin Whitten, hockey player and coach

Verna L. Williams, lawyer for Davis family against Monroe County Board of Education

Lee Wishing, director of college relations, Grove City College

Ron Wyden, U.S. senator

Ray Yasser, professor of law, University of Tulsa, and Title IX lawyer

for further information

BOOKS ABOUT GIRLS AND SPORTS

Blais, Madeleine. *In These Girls, Hope Is a Muscle: A True Story of Hoop Dreams and One Very Special Team.* New York: Warner Books, 1996.
A very entertaining and well-written tale of an Amherst, Massachusetts, high school team that shows the best of girls and sports.

Freedman, Russell. *Babe Didrikson Zaharias: The Making of a Champion.* New York: Clarion Books, 1999.
A thorough biography of this fascinating athlete.

Gottesman, Jane. *Game Face: What Does a Female Athlete Look Like?* New York: Random House, 2001.
A beautiful book celebrating females and sports.

Lannin, Joanne. *A History of Basketball for Girls and Women: From Bloomers to Big Leagues.* Minneapolis, MN: LernerSports, 2000.
A well-done chronicle of how the game of women's basketball has evolved over more than one hundred years.

Richardson, Dot, with Don Yaeger. *Living the Dream.* New York: Kensington Books, 1997.
A nicely told tale about her experiences in softball and life.

VanDerveer, Tara, with Joan Ryan. *Shooting from the Outside: How a Coach and Her Olympic Team Transformed Women's Basketball.* New York: Avon Books, 1997.
The story of the talented 1996 Olympic basketball team and a talented coach.

BOOKS ABOUT WOMEN'S RIGHTS

Bolden, Tonya, ed. *33 Things Every Girl Should Know About Women's History: From Suffragettes to Skirt Lengths to the E.R.A.* New York: Crown Publishers, 2002.
A collection of personal essays.

Davis, Flora. *Moving the Mountain: The Women's Movement in America Since 1960.* New York: Simon & Schuster, 1991.
This book is very long but very readable, with lots of stories.

Garza, Hedda. *Barred from the Bar: A History of Women and the Legal Profession.* New York: Franklin Watts, 1996.
A very detailed look at the women's movement and the fight for women to become lawyers.

Heinemann, Sue. *The New York Public Library Amazing Women in American History: A Book of Answers for Kids.* New York: John Wiley & Sons, 1998.

INFORMATION ABOUT TITLE IX

The Women's Sports Foundation, at www.womensportsfoundation.org, has lots of information on women, sports, and the latest issues regarding Title IX.

The NCAA has a Title IX section on its Web site, www.ncaa.org. It also has old articles and issues of its newsletter, the *NCAA News*, online going back to the 1970s.

The National Women's Law Center, at www.nwlc.org, has a wealth of reports and other up-to-date issues on Title IX as well as other women's issues.

The College Sports Council at www.savingsports.org takes a different look at the subject, from the perspective of wrestling, gymnastics, and swimming coaches.

A Hero for Daisy is a moving video about the Yale women's crew team. Information on the video as well as Title IX information is available at www.aherofordaisy.com.

USEFUL WEB SITES

The U.S. House of Representatives Web site for kids explains how a bill becomes a law, at www.clerkkids.house.gov.

A U.S. House of Representatives site on women in the House can be found at bioguide.congress.gov/congresswomen/index.asp.

A listing of government sites for kids is available at www.kids.gov.

photo credits

selected bibliography

Abzug, Bella. Edited by Mel Ziegler. *Bella! Ms. Abzug Goes to Washington*. New York: Saturday Review Press, 1972.

Ambrose, Susan A., Kristin L. Dunkle, Barbara A. Lazarus, Indira Nair, and Deborah A. Harkus. *Journeys of Women in Science and Engineering: No Universal Constants*. Philadelphia: Temple University Press, 1977.

Anderson, Dave. *The Story of the Olympics*. New York: HarperCollins Publishers, 2000.

Baker, Christina Looper, and Christina Baker Kline. *The Conversation Begins: Mothers and Daughters Talk about Living Feminism*. New York: Bantam Books, 1997.

Barrer, Myra E., ed. "Title IX—Prohibition of Sex Discrimination in Education," P. L. 92-318 (1972) *Journal of Reprints of Documents Affecting Women*, vol. 1, no. 1 (July 1976). Today's Publications and News Service Inc., Washington, D.C.

Bell, Terrel H. *The Thirteenth Man: A Reagan Cabinet Memoir*. New York: The Free Press, 1988.

Bernikow, Louise. *The American Women's Almanac: An Inspiring and Irreverent Women's History*. New York: Berkley Books, 1997.

Byers, Walter, with Charles Hammer. *Unsportsmanlike Conduct: Exploiting College Athletes.* Ann Arbor, Mich.: The University of Michigan Press, 1995.

Cahn, Susan K. *Coming on Strong: Gender and Sexuality in Twentieth-Century Women's Sport*. New York: The Free Press, 1994.

Califano, Joseph A., Jr. *Governing America: An Insider's Report from the White House and the Cabinet*. New York: Simon & Schuster, 1981.

Cooper, Cynthia. *She Got Game: My Personal Odyssey*. New York: Warner Books, 1999.

Davidson, Sue. *A Heart in Politics: Jeannette Rankin and Patsy T. Mink*. Seattle: Seal Press, 1994.

Davis, Flora. *Moving the Mountain: The Women's Movement in America Since 1960*. New York: Simon & Schuster, 1991.

DeCrow, Karen. *Sexist Justice: How Legal Sexism Affects You*. New York: Vintage Books, 1975.

Deford, Frank. *The Heart of a Champion: Celebrating the Spirit and Character of Great American Sports Heroes*. San Diego, Calif.: Tehabi Books, 2002.

Edwards, Lee. *Freedom's College: The History of Grove City College*. Washington, D.C.: Regnery Publishing, Inc., 2000.

Fischel, Andrew, and Janice Pottker. *National Politics and Sex Discrimination in Education*. Lexington, Mass.: Lexington Books, 1977.

Flexner, Eleanor. *Century of Struggle: The Women's Rights Movement in the United States*. Cambridge: Harvard University Press, Belknap Press, 1966.

Freedman, Russell. *Babe Didrikson Zaharias: The Making of a Champion.* New York: Clarion Books, 1999.

Friedman, Jane M. *America's First Woman Lawyer: The Biography of Myra Bradwell.* Buffalo, N.Y.: Prometheus Books, 1993.

Garza, Hedda. *Barred from the Bar: A History of Women and the Legal Profession.* New York: Franklin Watts, 1996.

Gelb, Joyce, and Marian Lief Palley. *Women and Public Policies.* Princeton, N.J.: Princeton University Press, 1982.

George, Emily S. *Martha W. Griffiths.* Lanham, Md.: University Press of America, 1982.

Green, Edith. *Fears and Fallacies: Equal Opportunities in the 1970s.* The Ninth Annual William K. McInally Memorial Lecture, given to the University of Michigan Graduate School of Business Administration, 1974.

Green, Edith. Interview by Cynthia E. Harrison. Dec. 18, 1978, for the Oregon Historical Society Research Library.

Green, Edith. Oral history interview by Shirley Tanzer. November 18, 1978–March 18, 1980. Sponsored by Former Members of Congress Inc. as part of "The Modern Congress in American History."

Griffiths, Martha W. Oral history interview by Emily George and Fern Ingersoll. December 1977–April 1978 and October 1979. Sponsored by Former Members of Congress Inc. as part of "The Modern Congress in American History."

Guttman, Allen. *Women's Sports: A History.* New York: Columbia University Press, 1991.

Hamm, Mia, with Aaron Heifetz. *Go for the Goal: A Champion's Guide to Winning in Soccer and in Life.* New York: HarperCollins Publishers, 1999.

Heinemann, Sue. *The New York Public Library Amazing Women in American History: A Book of Answers for Kids.* New York: John Wiley & Sons, Inc., 1998.

Hoose, Philip M. *Hoosiers: The Fabulous Basketball Life of Indiana.* York: Vintage Books, 1986.

———. *We Were There, Too!: Young People in U.S. History.* New York: Farrar Straus Giroux, 2001.

King, Billie Jean, with Kim Chapin. *Billie Jean.* New York: Harper & Row, 1974.

Lannin, Joanne. *A History of Basketball for Girls and Women: From Bloomers to Big Leagues.* Minneapolis, Minn.: LernerSports, 2000.

Leder, Jane. *Grace & Glory: A Century of Women in the Olympics.* Washington, D.C.: Multi-Media Partners Ltd. and Chicago: Triumph Books, 1996.

Levine, Suzanne, and Harriet Lyons, eds. *The Decade of Women: A Ms. History of the Seventies in Words and Pictures.* New York: G. P. Putnam's Sons, 1980.

Longman, Jere. *The Girls of Summer: The U.S. Women's Soccer Team and How It Changed the World.* New York: Perennial, 2000.

McGlen, Nancy E., and Karen O'Connor. *Women's Rights: The Struggle for Equality in the 19th and 20th Centuries.* New York: Praeger Publishers, 1983.

Millsap, Mary Ann. "Advocates for Sex Equity in Federal Education Law: The National Coalition for Women and Girls in Education." Ed.D. diss., Harvard University, 1988.

Mink, Patsy T. Oral history interview by Fern S. Ingersoll. March 6, March 26, June 7, 1979. Sponsored by Former Members of Congress Inc. as part of "The Modern Congress in American History."

Murphy, Irene L. *Public Policy on the Status of Women: Agenda and Strategy for the 70s.* Lexington, Mass.: Lexington Books, 1973.

The One Show: Advertising's Best Print, Radio, and TV, vol. 18 no. 113. New York: The One Club for Art and Copy, 1966.

President's Commission on the Status of Women. *American Women: The Report of the President's Commission on the Status of Women and Other Publications of the Commission.* New York: Charles Scribner's Sons, 1965.

Richardson, Dot, with Don Yaeger. *Living the Dream.* New York: Kensington Books, 1997.

Rosen, Ruth. *The World Split Open: How the Modern Women's Movement Changed America.* New York: Penguin Books, 2000.

Ross, Naomi Veronica. "Congresswoman Edith Green on Federal Aid to Schools and Colleges: A Thesis in Higher Education." Ed.D. diss., Pennsylvania State University, May 1980.

Schneir, Miriam. *Feminism in Our Time: The Essential Writings, World War II to the Present.* New York: Vintage Books, 1994.

Stimpson, Catharine R., ed. *Discrimination Against Women: Congressional Hearings on Equal Rights in Education and Employment.* New York: R. R. Bowker, 1973.

Stineman, Esther. *American Political Women: Contemporary and Historical Profiles.* Littleton, Col.: Libraries Unlimited, Inc., 1980.

Tinker, Irene. *Women in Washington: Advocates for Public Policy.* Beverly Hills, Calif.: Sage Publications, 1983.

Turco, Mary. *Crashing the Net: The U.S. Women's Olympic Ice Hockey Team and the Road to Gold.* New York: HarperCollins Publishers, 1999.

U.S. House Committee on Education and Labor. *Discrimination Against Women: Hearings before the Special Subcommittee on Education.* 91st Cong., Parts I & II.

Van Auken, Lance and Robin. *Play Ball! The Story of Little League Baseball.* University Park, Pa.: The University of Pennsylvania Press, A Keystone Book, 2001.

VanDerveer, Tara, with Joan Ryan. *Shooting from the Outside: How a Coach and Her Olympic Team Transformed Women's Basketball.* New York: Avon Books, 1997.

Ward, Geoffrey C., and Ken Burns. *Not for Ourselves Alone: The Story of Elizabeth Cady Stanton and Susan B. Anthony.* New York: Alfred A. Knopf, 1999.

Weinberger, Caspar W., with Gretchen Roberts. *In the Arena: A Memoir of the 20th Century.* Washington, D.C.: Regnery Publishing, Inc., 2001.

SELECTED PUBLICATIONS

Congressional Record
NCAA News
New York Times
Oregon Journal
The Oregonian
Sports Illustrated
Washington Post

index

a

b

c

n

National Aeronautics and Space Administration (NASA), 99
National Coalition for Women and Girls in Education, 71
National Collegiate Athletic Association (NCAA), 65, 71, 104–105, 121
National Education Association, 71
National Federation of Business and Professional Women, 71
National Federation of State High School Associations, 104
National Organization for Women (NOW), 20, 55, 71
National Wrestling Coaches Association, 119
Nike Inc., 114
Nineteenth Amendment, 11
Nixon, Richard, 32, 50, 51, 69
Norfolk Sports Club, 42

o

O'Connor, Sandra Day, 113
Olympic Games
  Atlanta 1996, 106–110
  Benoit in, 54
  de Varona and, 5, 7, 79, 94–95
  Didrickson at, 57–59
  Fernandez at, 93
  first women in, 54
  Los Angeles 1932, 57–59
  Los Angeles 1984, 94–95
  Richardson at, 45
  Tokyo 1964, 5, 7, 8
  winter 1998, 110
Osborne, Tom, 71

p

Paige, Rod, 120, 121
Parks, Missy, 80–81

Parks, Rosa, 14
Patsy Takemoto Mink Equal Opportunity in Education Act, 123
Pepe, Maria, 55
physical education instructors, 57
"Play Days," 57, 59
Polivy, Margot, 68, 72, 86–87
Princeton University, 37, 70
Professional Golf Association, 122–123
professional schools, 29–32, 33, 35, 37, 40, 49, 116. *See also* law schools, women in; medical schools, women in

q

Quindlen, Anna, 1
quotas, 30–31, 32, 37–40, 42, 70, 82, 85

r

racial discrimination, 14
Radcliffe College, 37
Reagan, Ronald, 89–90, 92, 93–94, 96, 98
Reid, Charlotte, 19
Rensselaer Polytechnic Institute, 116, 117
restoration bill, 96, 98
Retton, Mary Lou, 95
Reynolds, William Bradford "Brad," 92, 128
Richardson, Dorothy "Dot," 45, 91–92, 107–108, 109
Ride, Sally, 91, 98
Riggs, Bobby, 60–64, 93
rowing, 75–76
Royal, Darrell, 71, 72
Ryan, Mike, 95

s

Sandler, Bernice Resnick "Bunny," 29–32, 35, 72
Sanford, Terry, 86–87
Schembechler, Bo, 71, 72
Schlafly, Phyllis, 82